O'Connell

"Combining profound personal knowledge of prayer with a love of sacred scripture, Lohfink takes his readers on a journey through the vast wellspring that is Christian prayer. He focuses in particular on the Hebrew scriptures to demonstrate how sacred scripture is the word of the living God and the oldest faith-tradition of the church. In doing so, Lohfink demonstrates his erudition, facility, and reverence for the biblical texts. Throughout, Lohfink balances the particularity and variety of Christian prayer—from Trinitarian theology to the rosary to the eucharistic prayer—with the universality of worship of God and especially a deep respect for Judaism. Ultimately, for Lohfink, the most personal of prayers happens with and for the church and in communion with the body of Christ. This gorgeous book, rich in wisdom, will change the way readers understand and experience prayer."

> —Mahri Leonard-Fleckman
> Assistant Professor, Religious Studies
> College of the Holy Cross

"Rarely do you encounter in a spiritual work both brilliance and simplicity, a simultaneous honoring of the mystery and nearness of God, and words that positively contaminate your heart while challenging your mind. In Gerhard Lohfink's *Prayer Takes Us Home*, this is achieved. In today's anxious, uncertain world, we are challenged to see prayer more fully in ways that raise new questions as to how we can cooperate with God. This book reminded me of the works written by mystic and premier theologian, Karl Rahner. It is not the kind of book that you simply read. No. No. It also needs to be reflected upon, put down, and while the words are fresh in your mind, taken a walk with so you can come home to God in dynamic ways. If you take this book to heart it can be a portal to new joy and peace at a time when we need it most. The opportunity is there for you. I hope you avail yourself of it."

> —Robert J. Wicks
> Author, *Heartstorming: Creating a Place God Can Call Home*
> Editor, *Prayer in the Catholic Tradition*

"In *Prayer Takes Us Home*, Lohfink delights us with another refreshing exploration of Christian life and teaching—this time with a look at the central practice of prayer. In response to humble and practical questions about Christian prayer, Lohfink engages his life experiences and a wide range of interlocutors, from modern philosophers and great authors to our Jewish, Muslim, and Buddhist brothers and sisters. Yet *Prayer Takes Us Home* is always grounded in the close readings of scripture and attention to Christian tradition that are characteristic of Lohfink's writing. What results is a series of meditative essays that are deeply Christian and profoundly relevant to the lives of contemporary people of faith. Lohfink surprises readers with provocative observations and astute insights about this ancient practice, and as a result, opens our minds and spurs us to action."

—Jessica Coblentz
Saint Mary's College, South Bend, Indiana

*Gerhard Lohfink*

# Prayer Takes Us Home

## The Theology and Practice
## of Christian Prayer

Translated by

*Linda M. Maloney*

**LITURGICAL PRESS**
Collegeville, Minnesota

www.litpress.org

| 1 | 2 | 3 | 4 | 5 | 6 | 7 | 8 | 9 |
|---|---|---|---|---|---|---|---|---|

**Library of Congress Cataloging-in-Publication Data**

Names: Lohfink, Gerhard, 1934- author. | Maloney, Linda M., translator.
Title: Prayer takes us home : the theology and practice of Christian prayer / Gerhard Lohfink ; translated by Linda M. Maloney.
Other titles: Beten schenkt Heimat. English
Description: Collegeville, Minnesota : Liturgical Press, 2020. | Translation of: Gerhard Lohfink's Beten schenkt Heimat. Theologie und Praxis des christlichen Gebets, 2d ed. 2013, Verlag Herder GmbH, Freiburg im Breisgau. | Includes bibliographical references. | Summary: "Introduces the reader to the theology of prayer, referring again and again to the Bible, especially the Psalms. At the same time, it speaks about personal experiences"— Provided by publisher.
Identifiers: LCCN 2019053999 (print) | LCCN 2019054000 (ebook) | ISBN 9780814688069 (hardcover) | ISBN 9780814688311 (epub) | ISBN 9780814688311 (mobi) | ISBN 9780814688311 (pdf)
Subjects: LCSH: Prayer—Catholic Church. | Bible—Prayers—History and criticism.
Classification: LCC BV210.3 .L6413 2020 (print) | LCC BV210.3 (ebook) | DDC 248.3/2—dc23
LC record available at https://lccn.loc.gov/2019053999
LC ebook record available at https://lccn.loc.gov/2019054000

Dedicated to Peter F. Schneider
in gratitude

# Contents

# *Preface*

A lot of people want to learn how to pray again. Others are not sure whether they ought to pray at all. They want to know whether it helps them. More than that: they ask whether prayer makes any difference at all in our world.

This book tries to answer such questions, but not in the form of hasty recipes; instead, it leads us into the theology of prayer. Readers will quickly see that there is constant reference to the Bible, and especially the Psalms. But it is not just a book about the Psalms or about prayer in the Bible. For example, it is also about prayer in worship services and the basic structures of Christian meditation. Hence the subtitle: "The theology and practice of Christian prayer."

Be it noted: this book is not intended to offer a comprehensive or systematic doctrine of prayer. Rather, it tries to open paths by which people may advance in prayer or perhaps even dare to pray again. Readers will discover right away that it rests on many personal experiences; maybe that in itself will be helpful.

The immediate occasion for the book was a week-long course at the Academy of the People of God in the Villa Cavalletti near Rome from 1 to 7 July 2009. It was called "How Do We Pray as the People of God?" and there were a great many participants.

I remember those seven days in the Alban Hills with great pleasure—not only the lectures by Professor Georg Braulik, OSB, of Vienna, and by my brother, Professor Norbert Lohfink, SJ, of Frankfurt, but also the interaction of all the people there. In many discussions during the intermissions, at table, and in our excursion to Subiaco, the talk turned again and again to prayer and the theology of prayer.

My own lectures make up this book; nearly all of them have been reworked on the basis of suggestions and new ideas offered by Georg Braulik, my brother Norbert, and Professor Marius Reiser that I gratefully adopted. My special thanks to my former student, Dr. Linda M. Maloney, who has translated yet another of my books with her theological expertise and expert sense of the nuances of language.

I dedicate the book to Peter F. Schneider, who has gifted Christians with new songs of a high linguistic and musical quality. They breathe the spirit of the Psalms.

Gerhard Lohfink
Bad Tölz
12 September 2009

# On the Name of God

God's name in the Old Testament is YHWH. We have to add vowels to those four consonants (the Tetragrammaton) in order to speak the name. If we do so correctly, the original pronunciation of the name of God is not Jehovah but Yahweh. But Jews, out of reverence, do not utter that name. It is sacred to them. They paraphrase it as, for example, "the Name" (*Ha-shem*) or "Adonai" (the LORD). The Septuagint, the Greek translation of the Old Testament that is normative for Christians, accordingly translates YHWH as *Kyrios* (= Lord).

Christians need to respect the usage of their Jewish sisters and brothers, and consequently they should not utter the name of God either. In general I have used the word "Lord" wherever YHWH appears in the Hebrew text, and in small caps, thus: "LORD." There are, however, certain exceptions, namely, where the name of God is particularly emphasized in the Old Testament text or plays a decisive role. There I have left the Hebrew YHWH as it stands.

*Chapter 1*

# To Whom Do We Pray?

## A Sunday morning test

Suppose we are standing in front of a church on Sunday morning; the worship service has just ended. We approach as many of those coming out of the church as we can reach and ask them: "To whom were you praying during the service?" Certainly most of those questioned would be slightly irritated at first, and we could expect some evasive answers. But we would not let ourselves be discouraged, and we would stick to our question: "To whom were you praying?"

I am convinced that a large percentage of those questioned would say: "To God, of course. Who else?"—and that answer would be theologically wrong. Why? Because Christians do not pray to God; they pray either to God the Father or to Jesus Christ or to the Holy Spirit. Of course they believe in the *one* God and confess, with Israel, that there is but *one* God, but whenever they are praying to this God they address themselves to the Father, the Son, or the Holy Spirit.

## The basic movement of the liturgy

This is clear especially in the celebration of the Eucharist, in which we can read the substance of Christian faith and prayer. To whom does the church pray at Mass? The three "orations"—that is, the collect of the day, the prayer over the offerings, and the concluding prayer—are almost always addressed to God the Father.

The climax of the Mass, the Eucharistic Prayer, has the same basic structure. This great prayer, the primal model of all Christian prayers, is addressed to God the Father—*through* Christ *in* the Holy Spirit. The solemn conclusion of the prayer is:

> Through him [= through Christ], and with him, and in him,
> O God, almighty Father,
> in the unity of the Holy Spirit
> all glory and honor is yours,
> for ever and ever.
> Amen.

That is the obvious or hidden structural formula of all Christian prayers; it is the basic orientation of the whole liturgy, its fundamental movement: in the Holy Spirit, through Christ, to the Father.

Without calling that basic direction into question, the Mass also includes appeals to Jesus Christ: for example, the Kyrie or the second part of the Gloria, which is addressed to Christ, or the community's acclamation after the so-called "words of institution":

> We proclaim your Death, O Lord, and profess your Resurrection
> until you come again.

Similarly, the prayer for peace after the Our Father appeals to Christ:

> Lord Jesus Christ,
> who said to your Apostles:
> Peace I leave you, my peace I give you,
> look not on our sins,
> but on the faith of your Church,
> and graciously grant her peace and unity
> in accordance with your will.

Finally, we should mention also the prayer before communion when the congregation prays in words similar to those of the centurion at Capernaum:

> Lord, I am not worthy
> that you should enter under my roof,
> but only say the word
> and my soul shall be healed.

Even the orations (collects), the most strictly structured prayers of the Mass, can be addressed to Jesus Christ. Since the Middle Ages there have been a few collects in the Roman liturgy that do not address God the Father but speak directly to Christ. Because this prayer structure is so very rare I will quote an example from the Daily Office for the feast of Corpus Christi:

> [Lord Jesus Christ],[1] who in this wonderful Sacrament
> have left us a memorial of your Passion,
> grant us, we pray,
> so to revere the sacred mysteries of your Body and Blood
> that we may always experience in ourselves
> the fruits of your redemption.

Thus there are prayers in the Roman liturgy for the Mass in which Jesus Christ is directly addressed, and within the Mass formulary of the church's year there is even one prayer addressed to the Holy Spirit. It is the sequence for Pentecost, probably composed by Stephen Langton around the year 1200. This fully-formed work of art in Latin can only be inadequately reproduced in English:

> Come, Holy Spirit, come!
> And from your celestial home
> Shed a ray of light divine!
> Come, Father of the poor!
> Come, source of all our store,
> Come, within our bosoms shine.
> You, of comforters the best;
> You, the soul's most welcome guest;
> Sweet refreshment here below;
> In our labor, rest most sweet;
> Grateful coolness in the heat;
> Solace in the midst of woe.
> O most blessed Light divine,
> Shine within these hearts of thine,
> And our inmost being fill!
> Where you are not, we have naught,

---

1. The English translation (see, e.g., http://www.liturgies.net/Liturgies /Catholic/loh/loh.htm) begins paradoxically "O God." Translation LMM.

Nothing good in deed or thought,
Nothing free from taint of ill.
Heal our wounds, our strength renew;
On our dryness pour your dew;
Wash the stains of guilt away:
Bend the stubborn heart and will;
Melt the frozen, warm the chill;
Guide the steps that go astray.
On the faithful, who adore
And confess you, evermore
In your sevenfold gift descend;
Give them virtue's sure reward;
Give them your salvation, Lord;
Give them joys that never end.[2]

Still, these borderline exceptions do not change the basic orientation of liturgical prayer: to the Father through Christ. This fundamental movement of prayer was so important to the early church that in the year 393, at the Council of Hippo, it made it a strict rule:

*Semper ad Patrem dirigatur oratio.*
Prayer is always to be directed to the Father.

This brief look at the prayer structure of the Mass shows that the church never prays simply to God but always to the Father, the Son, or the Holy Spirit. It is very precise on this point. Unfortunately, when we pray privately we are not always so accurate. We often fail to make it clear to ourselves whom we are actually addressing in our prayer. We tell children we pray "to our dear God," and that idea endures, for the most part, in adults as well.

I am looking at a thick book, a collection of more than eight hundred prayers, most of them modern. It is called *The Big Book of Prayers*.[3] If we work through the book we see that the addressee of most of these prayers is unclear. Many begin with "God," or

---

2. *Veni, Sancte Spiritus*, from *The Roman Missal*, verses by Bob Hurd, arr. Craig Kingsbury (© 1964, US Conference of Catholic Bishops). Available at http://cdn.ocp.org/shared/pdf/preview/30126053.pdf.
3. *Das große Buch der Gebete* (Erftstadt: Hohe, 2007).

"Lord," which would be quite correct if it were made clear, within the prayer, that it is addressed to God the Father or to Jesus Christ, but mostly it is not, and it remains vague in the majority of the prayers; they lack contour. The error is certainly not the fault of the editors. Rather, they unwillingly document the fact that we have lost a part of our religious consciousness.

Here an essential part of Christian faith has been obscured and has lost the clarity it once had. The church, after all, does not believe in God *somehow or other*; it does not put its faith vaguely in a deity; it does not have a general belief in the divine or a reality that is foundational to the world. It believes in God the Father, the Almighty, the one who created us, and in Jesus Christ, the Son, who redeemed us, and in the Holy Spirit, who sustains the life of the church. Jean-Baptiste Noulleau (1606–1672), an Oratorian, rightly wrote:

> What can it profit anyone never to worship God except as "God," without thought of the trinity of divine Persons? If God had been invoked on a person in that way at baptism, the person would *not* be baptized. So if now that person does not call upon God in any other way, can she or he be a true Christian? Those who pray fully have a different attitude, making present not that God is God but that God is the "Father" . . . the God of Jesus Christ.[4]

## Face to face

When such faith expresses itself in prayer it has an almost alarming directness. Then we are really standing before God the Father, and as we call on the Father the whole history of this God with God's people since Abraham opens before us. It is only through this living confrontation that our worship services acquire their power and become infinitely more than a stage presentation about which we have to ask again and again, "Was everything well prepared, and did it all go according to plan?" Certainly worship services should be well prepared, but at some point there is a limit. As soon as it is reached we can forget about all the externals

---

4. As quoted in Henri Bremond, *Das wesentliche Gebet* [translation of *La Méta-physique des Saints*] (Regensburg: Pustet, 1959). English LMM.

because then only one thing matters: we are standing before the living God, the Father of Jesus Christ, and we are gathered in the Holy Spirit, the holy assembly of the church of God.

It is also because of this standing before the living God and God's story that our worship services are more than aesthetic arrangements. We do not gather primarily to enjoy music or the external forms of the liturgy or to hear a good sermon. The petitions we express do not function primarily to make us familiar with the needs of the world and so to sharpen our sense of responsibility.

Of course, it is lovely when the congregation sings well, when the organist has some talent, when the church space is pleasant, when the sermon has been carefully prepared and the petitions are appropriate. It is also a good thing when the worship service gives believers support and security in their lives and they go home edified.

But none of that is crucial. When Paul speaks of "building up" he means something different, something much greater and more important. He means that every worship assembly is to happen in such a way that the community is "built up" in the Holy Spirit to form the eschatological temple of God. We may also say that it is gathered into the form of society God wants it to be, and that happens first and foremost when it gives glory to God.

The congregation stands before God the Father in order to praise the Father together with Christ and to give thanks for God's saving deeds—and also, of course, to petition, that is, as a praying congregation to say "We cannot do it ourselves. We cannot live rightly. We cannot create a community. Of ourselves, we are not capable of anything good." Such asking and pleading is ultimately also a praise-filled acknowledgment of God. When praise and thanks offered to the Father constitute the basic movement of Christian worship, everything else happens almost by itself. Then "everything else"—namely, what the community needs for its concrete living—"will be given us besides."

## Moses on the mountain

There is a central text in the book of Exodus about this immediate standing before God. It is not altogether simple, but all the same I want to interpret it here. Readers need not be afraid: interpreting this text will demand something of them, but after that the book will get easier again. Still, it is worthwhile to take a closer look at this text in particular, because in it we find the basic structure of what prayer is in the Bible.

> ⁴So Moses . . . rose early in the morning and went up on Mount Sinai, as the LORD had commanded him. . . . ⁵The LORD descended in the cloud and stood with him there, and proclaimed the name, "The LORD." ⁶The LORD passed before him, and proclaimed,
>   "The LORD, the LORD,
>   a God merciful and gracious,
>   slow to anger,
>   and abounding in steadfast love and faithfulness. . . ."
> ⁸And Moses quickly bowed his head toward the earth, and worshiped. ⁹He said, "If now I have found favor in your sight, O Lord, I pray, let the Lord go with us. Although this is a stiff-necked people, pardon our iniquity and our sin, and take us for [your] inheritance." (Exod 34:4-9)

What is so striking about this text, which the NRSV translates as literally as possible, is the lack of clarity in the construction. First of all, in verse 5 God descends in the cloud. So far, so good. But who stands and calls out the name of the Lord? Since Moses is not introduced as a new subject, the hearer or reader simply assumes that it is God who stands beside Moses and proclaims the name of the Lord. In favor of this is also that then, in verse 8, Moses is introduced anew. It appears that God is still the subject in verses 5 and 6.

But if we read the text in that sense it is somewhat irritating. Why should God call out—or call on—God's own name? Besides: when the Old Testament uses the phrase "call on the name of the LORD" it is always a human being who is the subject. Still more: shortly before this, in Exodus 33:21, God has instructed Moses: "See, there is a place by me where you shall stand on the rock." Moses obeys that instruction in Exodus 34:5. Moreover, this text is echoed in Psalm 41: "you have . . . set me in your presence forever" (Ps 41:12).

It seems, then, that it is not God who is standing in the indicated place, but Moses. But then why is there no *clearly discernible* change of subject? Is this just lazy use of language? Or is there something more behind it?

The construction is unclear again in verse 6. The Lord passes by Moses and [a voice] calls out, "The Lord, the Lord." Who calls out? God or Moses? Again no new subject is introduced, but this time the matter is somewhat clearer because shortly before—in Exodus 33:18—Moses had asked to be allowed to see the divine glory. God had refused him because "no one shall see me and live." Instead, God will let the divine "goodness" pass before Moses:

> I will make all my goodness pass before you, and will proclaim before you the name, "The Lord"; and I will be gracious to whom I will be gracious, and will show mercy on whom I will show mercy. (Exod 33:19)

That makes it clear: at the moment when this promise is fulfilled in our text it is not Moses who cries out, "The Lord, the Lord"; it is God who calls out the divine name before Moses and reveals the divine mercy and graciousness.

Even so, some uncertainty remains because every person praying in and according to the Old Testament is accustomed to calling on God as "Lord." Hence there is a new irritant in verse 6: isn't it Moses, after all, who here calls on the name of the Lord and praises God, confessing God's compassion?

In both verses 5 and 6, then, the text creates uncertainties for the reader. Is it God who stands forth, or Moses? Is it God who speaks, or Moses? Are these the words *of God* or words addressed *to* God? Certainly a translator can easily smooth out the text simply by inserting a definite subject. But would that do justice to the biblical text? Is it ultimately ambiguous for a reason? Is it, in fact, deliberately irritating?

If the text really does intend such a thing it would not simply be an accident that it uses a formula for God's speaking that is otherwise only used to introduce human prayer, namely, "calling on the name of the Lord," or that it has God speak just as an Old Testament petitioner might speak, confessing "Lord, Lord." If God speaks here as a human being does when praying, it could mean that it was the narrator's intention to show God teaching Moses how to pray. We might say that for a moment God slips into the human role. In that case we can read the text of Exodus 34:4-9—among others—as teaching us how prayer should sound and what happens in true worship. Should we try it out? Let's read our text again, simply in those terms:

*Verses 4-5a*: Moses rises early in the morning and ascends Mount Sinai. So human beings must put themselves in motion, must go to meet God, must accept some cost. But this movement of the human toward God corresponds to a movement from God's side: God descends onto the mountain to meet Moses. Moses goes up and God comes down. Perhaps we should even say that God comes down to Moses because Moses goes up, or also the reverse: because God comes down to Moses, Moses can go up to God. Here is an indissoluble mutuality.

*Verse 5b*: God stands beside Moses, or Moses assumes a place close to God, a place God has shown him—after all, we saw that the text leaves the subject open. God is with Moses, and Moses is with God: encounter happens. Every prayer—especially every prayer of the assembled community—is a real encounter with God. But what does encounter mean in that context? It means that two persons, two freedoms, entrust themselves to one another without reservation, without fear and without hesitation.

*Verses 5c, 6*: God speaks the divine Name over Moses, the holy, inexpressible name Yhwh—or else Moses calls out the name of Yhwh. This means in the first place that God has a name, is a person, is a living partner, a Thou to whom one can speak. This is not Godhead in some vague sense, not a diffuse divinity.

It is important, of course, that the Name of God, God's true nature, the "Thou" we can address must be revealed directly by God. Therefore God calls out the divine name to Moses (v. 5), and therefore God reveals the divine nature by explaining the Name: "The Lord, the Lord, a God merciful and gracious, slow to anger, and abounding in steadfast love and faithfulness." And by leaving the subject open the text shows that this self-revelation of God culminates in Moses' appeal to God. Thus in every prayer God reveals the holy Name; that is: God reveals God's own self, and in every prayer, if it is genuine prayer, the one praying responds to this divine self-revelation by calling on the holy Name of God, praising and confessing it.

*Verses 5, 6*: Certainly God's self-revelation does not simply lead to a cozy companionship between God and the human being. As in every personal encounter the mystery remains, the hiddenness of the Other, the impassable gulf. Our text has two symbols for this:

First, the "cloud." It illustrates both hiddenness and incomprehensible nearness. We can enter into a cloud; it can surround us, but at the same time it occludes our sight altogether. Anyone who has climbed a peak and suddenly been fogged in can testify to that. And so can everyone who has ever struggled with God in prayer: God was near and yet always remained hidden.

The second symbol: God "passes by" Moses. God's face cannot be seen; God cannot be clung to. God cannot be harnessed to human purposes but must always withdraw again. Otherwise God would not be the holy God who is infinitely greater than everything we can imagine.

*Verses 8-9*: There can be only *one* reaction to this encounter with the holy God: adoration. Moses throws himself on the ground before God, but at the same time his adoration moves into petition. We could also say he throws himself on the ground in order to petition God, but his petition is simultaneously an adoring recognition of God.

For what does Moses pray? That the Lord who has passed by him and thereby revealed himself may accompany Israel and make it God's own possession, even though it is "a stiff-necked people." Isn't that also the basic structure of our worship? It is encounter with the holy God of Israel who is revealed in the divine Name and whom we dare call by name—that is, the God who is wholly and entirely personal. In prayer we dare stand before the face of God; we dare fall down before it; we dare call on God.

But do we also ask the most important thing Moses asks? He is no longer asking to be allowed to see God's glory (as in Exod 33:18-20) but requesting that the Lord will accompany Israel on its path through the wilderness and make it God's own people. Evidently the first and most important theme of all our prayers must be on behalf of the People of God: that God may gather it, lead it, protect it, and care for it, even though it is a stiff-necked and sinful people.

Let us conclude this examination of Exodus 34:4-9 by returning to the ambivalence of the construction in verses 5 and 6. Evidently it is deliberate: it intends to leave open whether *God* calls out the divine Name or *Moses* appeals to it. Thus God enters into the role of the one praying—or, to put it another way: God teaches us *in person* how we should pray. And precisely that is an extraordinarily important point in any theology of prayer. We could state it this way:

> We ourselves cannot pray. We do not know what prayer is and most certainly not what we should pray for if our prayer is to be genuine. God, in person, has to teach us about prayer. Still more: God must pray in us, and we can enter into God's prayer. But how can it be that God prays in us? How can one and the same person turn with ultimate surrender to the self and the result not be an unbearable *self-centeredness*?

## The Spirit's sighing

If we consider that question more deeply, our discontent with Exodus 34:4-9 almost inevitably leads us to the question of the three Persons in God, because if God prays in us, and if that *prayer of God in us* is to be worthy of the holy God, then we have to think of God as a conversation. Can we really think that? Or are we here falling into the quicksand of meaningless speculation? No, such a thing is thinkable. Paul himself thought in just that direction; after all, in Romans 8:26-27 he wrote:

> Likewise the Spirit helps us in our weakness; for we do not know how to pray as we ought, but that very Spirit intercedes with sighs too deep for words. And God [= God the Father], who searches the heart, knows what is the mind of the Spirit, because the Spirit intercedes for the saints according to the will of God.

First we have to consider the context within which Paul wrote those sentences. He had already spoken at Romans 8:22 about "sighing": all creation lies in birth pangs. It sighs and groans because it is not what, in God's mind, it ought to be. Because of the human history of sin it is subjected to nothingness and mortality. What human beings do always leaves its mark on their environment. When they destroy themselves they destroy creation along with them.

So creation groans and sighs—and so do humans. They suffer together with the creation they have destroyed, and they too, like creation, need to be freed and redeemed. Even the baptized live under the pressure of suffering that lies upon creation. They too groan and sigh and await their liberation. It is true that—unlike those who do not believe—they are filled with hope, for in baptism they have already received the Holy Spirit as the beginning of eschatological salvation. The Spirit "dwells" in the baptized (Rom 8:9, 11), but for that reason the discrepancy between the preliminary gift of the Spirit and the redemption that still awaits is all the greater.

After all, Christians speak of redemption, liberation, and future glory, but they cannot grasp what those words really express. They are part of the still invisible gifts of salvation (Rom 8:25) that are greater than anything a human being can imagine. Hence Christians (and this, of course, is still more true of pagans) are ultimately incapable of prayer: they cannot bridge the profound discrepancy between the Holy Spirit, already received, and the salvation yet to come. Their prayer cannot sustain the tension between the reality in which they live and the salvation already given them. Christians utter many words in prayer, but those words cannot touch God's reality. The New Testament scholar Heinrich Schlier (1900–1978) wrote correctly of our text: "Our sighing (and longing), no matter how internalized, never comprehend what is being called for."

In this crisis the Holy Spirit comes to the aid of the baptized, representing those praying before God the Father. Paul had already written (in Rom 8:15) that it is *through the Holy Spirit* who has made them sons and daughters of God that the baptized cry, "Abba, Father." Thus it is already clear that there is no genuine prayer that does not take place through the Holy Spirit. Our text renders this idea still more profound: The Holy Spirit, in person, speaks to the Father in the baptized, in whom the Spirit dwells, "with sighs too deep for words."

So Paul again takes up the phrase about the groaning and sighing of creation. The Holy Spirit, by sighing, adopts and owns the sighing of suffering people. But at the same time the Spirit speaks in sighs *too deep for words*, sighs that are *inexpressible*. This means that the Spirit transforms our sighing—for example, when we complain to God—into the language that is "worthy of" and appropriate for God, the language we cannot command. This is a conversation within God's self.

## A visit to Aristotle

But what kind of conversation is that? At this point it is worth our while to pay a visit to the great philosopher Aristotle (384–322 BCE). For him, God is perfect spirit existing from eternity from and through itself. God is pure spirit, pure thought. "But then what does God think?" Aristotle asks in the twelfth book of his *Metaphysics* (1074b), and he answers: God thinks *God's self*—presuming that God is really the highest being. What else could God think, according to Aristotle's logic? God is perfect being-in-itself. If God were to think something other than God, such as human beings or the world or any individual things, God would no longer be thinking of the highest thing and thus would voluntarily move out of God's self and lose divine perfection.

Christian theology gratefully made use of Greek philosophy, thinking of God in Aristotle's categories, and yet it went far beyond Aristotle. From the beginning it was aware that God thinks not only God's self but the world. Moreover: God speaks not only within God's self; God speaks the eternal divine Word into the world. Still more than that: God creates the world from the beginning through that eternal Word that is Christ. And finally: God sends the divine Spirit to renew the world so that it can enter into dialogue with God. It is precisely because God sends the eternal Word and the Holy Spirit into the world to dwell there that God can think the world.

Thus conversation in God does not revolve around itself, any more than God thinks only God; rather, that conversation grasps the world and comprehends it. The baptized are empowered to say, "Abba, Father," with Jesus and, in the Holy Spirit, to speak to the Father in sighs too deep for words.

God is not only self-possession, as Aristotle thought, but self-gift. The Father's self-surrender is continued in the self-surrender of the

Son and the self-exhalation of the Holy Spirit. It is precisely in this that God possesses the divine Self and thinks God through self-surrender. Out of love, in the Father's surrender to the Son and the Holy Spirit, God thinks the world, calls it into being, and enters into conversation with it. Indeed, through that conversation God creates it and constantly creates it anew. Every prayer must be thought of on this basis, in terms of this trinitarian primal movement.

Ultimately, then, prayer means entering into the conversation among Father, Son, and Holy Spirit—not out of our own power and ability, but empowered by being made sons and daughters in baptism. Every adequate theology of prayer must lead to this insight and has already done so. As an example of many possible citations I have chosen a passage from the book *Instructions for Those Who Find It Difficult to Pray*,[5] by the Franciscan Oratorian Claude Séguenot (1634):

> How can we achieve anything through the natural strength of our spirit? What community is there between it and God? The Holy Spirit teaches us to pray. But that is not saying enough. [The Spirit itself] prays in us, lifts up our spirit, encourages our will, breathes sighs into our hearts and makes us serve God rightly—and more: [The Spirit itself] serves God for us. It is not you who pray. Prayer is not the work of the human spirit. The smaller our own share in it, the better we pray.

So we can return to our initial thesis. It should be clear by now that our prayer cannot and must not be vaguely directed toward God. It is addressed either to God the Father or to Jesus Christ or to the Holy Spirit. Ultimately, however, it is always directed *in* the Holy Spirit, *through* Christ, *to* the Father. The liturgy, and especially the Eucharistic Prayer, shows us this basic process of Christian prayer.

But if that is the case, if we can never pray except to the Father, the Son, or the Holy Spirit, isn't there a great danger that we will

---

5. *Conduite d'oraison, pour les âmes qui n'y ont pas facilité* (Paris: S. Huré, 1663). English LMM, from the German translation, *Anweisungen für das Gebet solcher, die Mühe damit haben*, as quoted in Henri Bremond, *Das wesentliche Gebet: La Métaphysique des Saints*, trans. Hedwig Michel (Regensburg: Pustet, 1936), 93.

worship them as three gods? How can we explain to a believing Jew or a pious Muslim that such is not the case? On this account we must take another step, one that I dare not simply avoid. We have to ask: what exactly does theological language about three persons in God mean?

## The reproach of Islam

In our present situation it is more important than ever to reflect on God in three persons, because in recent decades Islam has been spreading more powerfully than anyone would have imagined in the first half of the twentieth century. Islam regards Africa as "its own" part of the earth. There are more active Muslims in France than active Christians. In Berlin, every year, more children are born into Muslim families than are baptized as Christians. A steady stream of Muslim missionaries passes through Vienna's airport to support the Islamic mission in Austria. The main theme of their preaching is that Christians have falsified Scripture, falling into polytheism and thus idolatry. They worship three gods.

This accusation was central to Islam from the beginning. Mohammed fought first against the older Arabian polytheism, but he very quickly turned also against Christian belief in the triune God. The famous *Sura* 112 in the Qur'an reads:

> Say: "He is Allah, the One and Only;
> Allah, the Eternal, Absolute;
> He begets not, nor is He begotten.
> And there is none like unto Him.[6]

This may well have been spoken directly against the Christian doctrine of the Trinity. Saying that God does not beget is an attack on the Christological confession "begotten, not made." *Sura* 4.48 avers that polytheism of that sort is an unforgivable sin:

---

6. Quotations from the Qur'an are taken from *The Qur'an*, trans. Abdullah Yusuf Ali, 20th ed. (Elmhurst, NY: Tahrike Tarsile Qur'an, Inc., 2007).

Allah does not forgive that partners should be set up with Him;
but He forgives anything else, to whom He pleases; to set up
partners to Allah is to devise a sin most heinous indeed.

That too is directed primarily against Christians. There is but one
sin that Allah will never forgive, so it says. All other sins he can, in
his mercy, set aside, but the sin of setting other gods alongside the
*one* God he can never forgive. If that is what Christians do, then
Muslims who take their own tradition seriously must maintain that
Christians are idolaters for whom there is no pardon for all eternity.

## The experience of history

But Christians do not worship three gods! They explicitly confess
faith in the *one* God, the God of Abraham, Isaac, and Jacob. Worship of the triune God does *not* mean that there are three gods;
rather, it says that all honor, all worship, all praise belongs to God
the Father. But at the same time worship of the triune God affirms
that ultimately the Father can only be known and glorified through
the Son and in the Holy Spirit. How did this way of worshiping
God come about, with its basis in Israel, in its foundational, utterly
radical monotheism?

First of all, there is the experience of the Old Testament People
of God with the one God who brought this people out of Egypt,
traveled with them through the wilderness, led them, rescued
them, forgave their sin, and is near and alongside them. This is no
absent, rejecting, distant god. This is a close, saving God, a God
who comes to the aid of God's people. Israel itself gives this God
the loveliest name God can have, calling God its "Father."

This basic experience of nearness that Israel has always had
with its God acquired a new dimension in Jesus. In him God has
now definitively been made present in the midst of God's people.
Jesus' disciples could not say it any other way. They had to say that
Jesus is God's ultimate, definitive Word in whom God has communicated God's self entirely, communicated everything forever
and definitively acted. In short: whoever sees Jesus sees the Father.
And because Jesus is wholly the image, wholly the reflection of

the Father, they had to say Jesus is the "Son." That does *not* mean he is a "second" god but that he is the definitive presence of the Father in the world. Hence from then on the prayer of the People of God can no longer ignore him. All prayer to the God of Israel now takes place "with him" and "in his name."

Then, at Pentecost, all that is made more profound through a third fundamental experience: Jesus is—superficially—no longer present. His disciples can no longer see him. No one can hear him any longer. And yet he is not separated from his disciples; he is in their midst. He is among them when they gather. In fact, he is closer to them than he ever had been. He is with them through his Spirit. This is the fundamental experience of Easter and Pentecost and of the church as a whole: Jesus is present in the Holy Spirit, and with Jesus the Father also.

If the church no longer talks in undifferentiated fashion about God, but instead speaks of "Father," "Son," and "Spirit," that is not an afterthought, nor is it an ideology directed against Israel's monotheistic faith. That would, historically speaking, be altogether unlikely because the experiences we have described happened in Israel's midst, that is, within the sphere of the strictest imaginable monotheism.

Those who formulated the belief in the triune God were not Gentile Christians but Jews, deeply rooted in Israel's faith. And the theologians who, in subsequent centuries, plunged more deeply into the mystery of the triune God in order to secure it against misunderstandings were not thinking in the spirit of Greek philosophy. In that case they would have had to speak in Neo-platonic fashion of the "primeval One," the negation of all multiplicity. No, they did not think in terms of Hellenistic speculation about gods but in light of the New Testament.

Thus faith in the Father, Son, and Spirit rests on historical experience in which God has revealed God's own self. The *one* God has become a presence in the world in a way that has led all previous divine becoming-present to its goal and perfection. Therefore the Son and Spirit are not two new gods but the revelation and caring concern of the one God for the world, in which God is altogether with it—in the face of the Son and the power of the Spirit. None of that has anything to do with polytheism, not in the slightest;

what it is about is the incomprehensible and superabundant love of God for the world.

Prayer can no longer avoid facing this ultimate speaking and act-ing of God in history. A prayer completely decoupled from that, not directed through Christ to the Father in the Holy Spirit, but only to God in a vague sense, would deny the historical basis of Christian be-lief. To put it as bluntly as possible: it would no longer be Christian.

## Church as reflection of the triune God

We must ask ourselves, of course: why has this truth about the three-person God and God's historical self-revelation become so foreign to people today—not only the neo-pagans, but many Christians as well?

It is probably connected with the fact that the Holy Spirit has become or remained a stranger to them—and with the Holy Spirit what community, or church, is. It is true that the Holy Spirit is hard to picture, but there does exist a reflection of the Spirit. Certainly I have never been able to do much with the dove—above all because my study of behaviors has shown me that doves can be quite un-pleasant. No, the true image of the Holy Spirit is the church, the Christian community with its assemblies. An assembled congre-gation seeking the will of God, with one mind, attentive to every individual and making something of the love of God visible: that is the most beautiful reflection of the Holy Spirit. Such an as-sembly can be seen at a glance to be different from a gathering of Christians who are stiff and unfree, or disunited and in conflict.

So Luke is right to show in his Pentecost narrative that the Holy Spirit is *perceptible*. We can see very quickly whether an assembly is driven by the Spirit of God or by some other spirit. God wills the world and wants to be very, very close to this world; God wants to dwell within it. The place of God's presence is the community of believers. There Jesus is present, and there his Holy Spirit can fill and fulfill all. That is why it is precisely there, in the unified single-hearted community, that one can experience the triune God.

People are by nature very different. We each have our own ori-gins, our own history, our own insights and points of view. When, in spite of all this often profound difference, people become a unified, single-minded congregation we can get a little taste of what the triune God is: difference of persons and yet unity in nature; an unceasing conversation that takes place in love.

## Shared life

Therefore faith in the one God, who is yet triune, has not only a historical but also a social basis. The insight that God, in three persons, is one God is not just one among many possibilities. It is given where the People of God itself lives as a *communio*—where believers trust one another, accept one another in mutual *agapē*, and share their lives with one another. The insight that God is a triune being-together presumes the being-together of the community itself. This insight presupposes church, community, assemblies in which there are many different persons and yet the unanimity of all.

Our image of God is, in fact, always socially conditioned. A society full of violence will believe in a violent god. For a society whose principle of unity is absolutist power, God must also be an absolutist ruler.

By contrast, a society that lives in a community of trust and unanimity will receive the revelation of the true triune God. There the Holy Spirit can be recognized as the personal bond in love. Where Christians share their lives with one another they can at least surmise that there is also a shared life in God, a mutually self-giving life. When these experiences are no longer present there is a danger that confession of the Trinity will become purely formulaic.

Consequently, the history of continually deeper experience of the true God is simultaneously a long stretch of human social history. It was only in the moment when, in the course of evolution of social forms, a form of *communio* was achieved in the primitive community in Jerusalem, where a social group was held together not through power or force but through unanimity and trust in a shared life—only then could the Spirit of God be recognized as a divine Person and God be known as a three-person God.

Therefore the feast of Pentecost—the birthday of the eschatological People of God—is the hour in which the Holy Spirit was definitively recognized, and with it the triune God. For in the wake of the feast of Pentecost it could be said:

> All who believed were together and had all things in common. . . . Day by day, as they spent much time together in the temple, they broke bread at home and ate their food with glad and generous hearts. (Acts 2:44, 46)

Just as the entire search for the true God found its definitive home in Jesus Christ, so all searching for the Spirit of God has its definitive place in the Pentecost community. Consequently the Pentecost church is at the same time the social basis for recognizing the triune God.

In turn, of course, it is also true that where people live in and on the basis of adoration of the triune God what we call society changes as well: a conversation can become speechless. Egoists can surrender themselves to a cause that is far greater than themselves and makes them suddenly focus on the happiness of *others*. But above all: people who are fundamentally different by their very nature can come together, find agreement, become a unity without any damage to their freedom—and all that not from their own strength, not through human effort, but through grace. It is given them as a reflection of the life of the triune God.

## Three persons in God

The primary and most profound reason for difficulty with the Christian doctrine of the Trinity is thus the absence of any genuine experience of church. The second reason is what we will speak of next: that many people have a wrong idea of what is meant by the three "persons" in God; that is, they do not know what the language of the church's faith means by "person."

What is a person? In our naïve, prescientific understanding we see every adult person as a complete, autonomous reality that exists for itself. This compact, sharply distinguished reality then also makes contact with other realities of the same kind, that is, other persons. If we imagine the triune God in that form we of course have three gods, certainly in relationship with each other but each of them in the first place a self-contained reality.

Even in the case of human beings as persons, however, the idea of a sharply distinguishable reality is only partly correct, because as regards a human being the question is: insofar as this is a person, is she or he really such an autonomous, independent reality existing within itself?

To put it very simply: how, then, does the child that develops from embryo to adult become a person? I am not posing a theological question about the "nature" of a child. The issue is clear for Christian faith: every human being is a person from the first second of its existence because it is seen and loved by God. No, I am asking the phenomenological question: How does the initial clump of cells become *the* person whom we encounter, many years later, as an adult?

A development takes place—indeed, an extraordinarily long and subtle development. A seemingly infinite series of things must happen. We cannot begin to list everything that goes into the making of a person. The child must be nourished and cared for. Its parents have to smile at it. Above all: they must speak with it. And the child is constantly expanding the number of faces it recognizes. It becomes increasingly intertwined in a thick web of relationships: first with its parents, then with other children, then with a steadily growing number of adults.

The language a child slowly learns conveys a world to it. The care bestowed on it by its parents and many others is what creates primal trust, the basic precondition for real human personhood. The child enters into a more and more intensive relationship to the world. It takes in more and more of the world and shapes a world of its own. It builds a world around it and internalizes it.

So what is a person? It is not merely a reality resting in and focused on itself but always also the sum of its relationships to other people and to the world. This is most fully visible in love, the turning of the self to another Thou, entrusting oneself, surrendering oneself. Every human person is thus self-existing but is also to an extraordinary degree "relational"—and much more intensively so than we normally acknowledge. We usually think that we exist entirely within ourselves, but that is not true.

Now let us make the counter-experiment: we will eliminate from the history of our lives all the people we have ever met or had anything to do with: mother, father, spouse, siblings, friends, acquaintances, neighbors, all our teachers. We also eliminate all the books we have ever read, all the media that have instructed us, all the things that have fascinated us, all the conflicts we have entered into, everything in the world we have ever encountered.

What remains of us? Only a torso, an empty shell, a clump of cells, a skeleton. In other words, being a person means essentially *being-in-relationship*. Without the web of relationships in which we have lived in the past and in which we live today we would be nothing.

And now the theology of the triune God tells us: the Father, Son, and Spirit are pure, self-existent relationships. They are *not* self-enclosed realities but, insofar as they are persons, nothing but relational, that is, relationships. The Father is pure self-communication and self-giving to the Son. The Son is pure listening to the Father. The Spirit is pure receptiveness to Father and Son. As a whole the one God is an absolute "we" unimaginable to us. So the mystery of the triune God makes it clear to us that the ultimate is not being-in-itself, being-for-itself, but being-for-another and being-from-another.

To make this decisive difference in the trinitarian concept of person still clearer we may consider ourselves once again. I am I, my "ego," my self: I do something. I stand, I sit, I walk around the room, I eat, I go to bed in the evening. "I" do all that. But I am not simply identical with what I do. I am not simply my standing or eating, nor am I simply my going-to-bed. There always remains an acting center that does or does not do certain things.

But the theology of the three divine Persons says that in them such a difference does not exist. God the Father is not first of all God the Father, who then does something else: loving. No, Sacred Scripture tells us that God is love (1 John 4:8). This means that loving is not something extra added to the Father; instead, the Father is nothing other than the event of purely loving. In exactly the same way the Son is nothing other than pure listening, pure receiving, pure handing on of what is heard from the Father (John

15:15). Correspondingly, the Holy Spirit is nothing other than pure receiving and being the bond of love between Father and Son.

I think it is clear that when we speak of three *Persons* in God the concept of "person" we are using is completely different from the idea of personhood we apply to ourselves. We cannot conceive a positive idea of the personhood of Father, Son, and Holy Spirit. Indeed, that is true of everything we say of God: we can speak of God only in images and comparisons in which the dissimilarity is infinitely greater than the similarity. Even when we speak of *three* Persons we have to be clear that the number "three" is only an analogous concept: it is something completely different from saying "three trees" or "three houses" or "three people."

And despite all this we may pray to Father, Son, and Holy Spirit. We may and must stand before their face and address them in prayer, because they are much more intensely and more gloriously Person than we can begin to conceive what a "person" is.

Clearly, we dare not approach such a mystery altogether in terms of concepts. The only adequate form of approach to this God is praise—praising the truth that the triune God desires from all eternity to receive us into that community and give us a share in the eternal divine life that is nothing but love.

## A difficulty

I do not want to conclude this first chapter, which is so basic for Christian prayer, without discussing a difficulty that is "in the air," as we might say. I can imagine someone posing the following objection:

> That is all too complicated for me. Until now I have always simply prayed to *God*, and I want to go on doing that. It would be unbearable to me to have to think, every time, that I am praying in the Holy Spirit through Jesus Christ to the Father. It would destroy the immediacy and simplicity of my prayer. The thoughts presented here may be important to theologians but they have nothing to do with real life. Besides, preachers and even theologians mostly talk simply about "God" without

constantly making distinctions. So I'm going to go on praying
to *God* and no one else.

The objection is understandable, but it is off the mark. Karl
Rahner, in one of his important essays, investigated the concept
of "God" in the New Testament. He was able to show that in
the vast number of passages in which the word "God" appears
in the New Testament it almost always refers to God the Father.
"God" never refers to the trinitarian God in three persons. That
New Testament usage endured for a long time in the practice of
the ancient church. It appears, for example, in the ancient Roman
baptismal confession (the source of the so-called Apostles' Creed),
which says:

> I believe in God, the Father almighty . . .
> and in Jesus Christ, his only Son . . .
> and in the Holy Spirit . . .

This rule of speech did not mean, of course, that Jesus Christ
and the Holy Spirit are not true God just as the Father is. But the
language attaches "God" to the Father. It was only the usage of
medieval Scholastic theology that changed that—in the West. From
then on the word "God," when used without further qualification,
often meant the trinity of Persons as a whole. But as we saw at the
beginning of this chapter, the liturgy held to the old usage. For example, in the collect for the Twentieth Sunday of the year it prays:

> O God, who have prepared for those who love you
> good things which no eye can see,
> fill our hearts, we pray, with the warmth of your love,
> so that, loving you in all things and above all things,
> we may attain your promises,
> which surpass every human desire.
> Through our Lord Jesus Christ, your Son . . .

In the Latin of this and many other collects the address is simply
*Deus*, that is, "God." But in the course of the prayer and above
all through the doxology at the end it becomes clear that "God"
here refers to none other than God the Father. It is time for this

understanding of the language to be restored. It is good biblical language, and it has the church's tradition behind it.

With regard to the objection voiced above, this means that when we pray we may simply say "God." We only need to recall from time to time that it almost always means God the Father and that the direction of the prayer should also be expressed in some way by the content of the prayer itself.

We don't have to remember constantly that we are praying *through* Jesus Christ *in* the Holy Spirit. It is enough to have reflected thoroughly on this profound mystery at least once in the course of our lives. Likewise the liturgy, with its doxologies, constantly reminds us of this basic structure of all prayer.

In the end we need to know that because ultimately we are always praying to God, our Father, we are thereby united not only with Jesus, who taught us to pray, "Abba, dear Father," but also most profoundly with Israel and Judaism. Israel is the olive tree into which we Gentile Christians have been grafted.

*Chapter 2*

# God Is Acting Today

## The vicar of Savoy

*[handwritten annotation: intercessory prayer unneeded]*

The year 1762 saw the publication of Jean-Jacques Rousseau's great novel about education, *Émile.*[1] Within the novel a vicar from Savoy appears and presents his thoughts on God and the world in a kind of creed. It is a long speech, and of course it is Rousseau who is addressing the reader in it. One part of the speech is about prayer, and there we read:

> I consider the order of the universe, not to explain it by any futile system, but to revere it without ceasing, to adore the wise Author who reveals himself in it. I hold intercourse with him; I immerse all my powers in his divine essence; I am overwhelmed by his kindness, I bless him and his gifts, but I do not pray to him. What should I ask of him—to change the order of nature, to work miracles on my behalf? Should I, who am bound to love above all things the order which he has established in his wisdom and maintained by his providence, should I desire the disturbance of that order on my own account? No, that rash prayer would deserve to be punished rather than to be granted. Neither do I ask of him the power to do right; why should I ask what he has given me already? Has he not given me conscience that I may love the right, reason that I may perceive it, and freedom that I may choose it? . . . Thou source of justice and truth, merciful

---

1. *Émile, ou, de l'éducacion* (many editions). English: *Emile* (n.p.: CreateSpace Independent Publishing Platform, 2016), 140.

and gracious God, in thee do I trust, and the desire of my heart is—Thy will be done. When I unite my will with thine, I do what thou doest; I have a share in thy goodness; I believe that I enjoy beforehand the supreme happiness which is the reward of goodness.

I cannot go into the details of this text at present, nor do I want to describe the religious system within which it stands. I have only quoted *Émile* in order to make it clear that this is not fundamentally a rejection of prayer; indeed, the vicar of Savoy prays constantly to God. He praises God, full of wonder at God's works, and at the end of the text just quoted his speech is transformed into prayer itself. What he rejects, however, is prayer of petition. He does so because it asks God to intervene in the life of the world for the sake of the one praying. That would not accord with God's wise ordering of the world. How could God, who created a world system perfect in itself, go around correcting parts of that system—only because such a thing is demanded by humans who lack understanding?

At the point where Rousseau's speech about God is transformed into a prayer to God, however, there are two statements that at first glance seem contradictory: "in thee do I trust, and the desire of my heart is—Thy will be done. When I unite my will with thine, I do what thou doest."

"Thy will be done" sounds altogether biblical. It is an allusion to the third petition of the Our Father, which asks that God accomplish the divine will to salvation in the world, that is, that God will intervene in the world. Is Jean-Jacques Rousseau inconsistent at this point? No! He thinks of "the will of God" not as God's saving will that is active in history; rather, he means the eternal, unchanging will of the Creator that sustains the universe. And God never interferes in the course of the universe.

Rousseau is in agreement with many other great minds of the Enlightenment in thus rejecting the prayer of petition, but Rousseau's skill with language enabled him to formulate his objection in a way that had the maximum effect. We can no longer imagine the fascination that *Émile* had for Rousseau's contemporaries. It entranced them and led them astray. Certainly the majority of Enlightenment authors went much further than Rousseau, categorically rejecting *any* kind of prayer, and they despised Rousseau's vicar of Savoy.

## Morality instead of prayer

Some thirty years later Immanuel Kant wrote his famed and influential book *Religion within the Bounds of Bare Reason.*[2] There, in the "General Comment" preceding the "Fourth Piece," he wrote:

> 1. *Praying*, conceived as an *inward formal* service of God and hence as a means of grace, is a superstitious delusion (a fetishism). For, it is a mere *declaration of wishing* [literally 'declared wishing'] directed toward a being that needs no declaration of the inward attitude of the person wishing; thus nothing is done through it and therefore none of the duties incumbent upon us as commands of God are performed, and hence God is not really served.

The context makes it clear that what Kant intends to say is that what matters is one thing only: living a life pleasing to God. For that, our "moral sense" must be continually purified. At most, prayer serves to enliven that right attitude in us. But better than any prayer is the "contemplation of the profound wisdom of divine creation." Prayer can disappear entirely if a proper moral sensibility can be achieved by some other means.

So Kant leaves some room for prayer on the margins—if, that is, it leads the person praying to a right sensibility and to the actions that duty requires. It is still useful as a means of changing attitudes and of motivating people to moral action. But prayer as "formal worship" is senseless and even dangerous, because then it too easily becomes a substitute, taking the place of real moral action.

Because Kant has exercised such an immense influence in intellectual history he, of course, impressed many theologians as well.

2. *Die Religion innerhalb der Grenzen der blossen Vernunft* (1st ed., 1793; 2nd ed., 1794), 194–95, 197. Quoted here from the translation by Werner S. Pluhar (Indianapolis: Hackett, 2009), 215–16, 218.

For Albrecht Ritschl (1822–1889), who decisively influenced German Protestant theology well into the twentieth century, no prayer of petition is appropriate. In his book *Instruction in the Christian Religion*[3] he explains that only thanksgiving and praise are worthy of God. Petition is contrary to God's will.

Naturally, this thesis produced massive problems for Ritschl—beginning with the Our Father. He could only escape the dilemma by declaring it to be purely a prayer of thanksgiving and praise, but that wouldn't wash. The Our Father is pure petition.

## Mother Courage

My purpose is certainly not to write a history of the rejection of prayers of petition. I would like to recall just one more text, namely, Bertolt Brecht's *Mother Courage and Her Children*.

In the eleventh scene of the play it is night; the imperial troops are approaching the town of Halle. In a farmhouse outside the city the soldiers are trying to force a group of peasants to show them a secret way into the city. The peasants are unable to do anything but wail and pray:

> Our Father, which art in Heaven, hear our prayer, let not the town perish with all what are in it and slumbering and don't know nothing. Wake them, that they get up and go onto the walls and see how they are coming at them with pikes and cannons in the night down the slope and across the fields. . . .

> . . . Make the watchman not sleep but wake; otherwise it'll be too late. And be with our son-in-law, too, O God, he's in there with his four children, let them not perish, they're innocent, they don't know nothing. . . .

> Our Father, hear us, only Thou canst help us, we're like to die, why, we are weak and have no pike nor nothing; we can't do nothing for ourselves and are in Thy hand, our cattle, our farm,

---

3. *Unterricht in der christlichen Religion* (1st pub., 1875; many editions).

and the town too, it's in Thy hand, and the foe is before the walls with mighty power.[4]

While the peasants are praying, Kattrin, the mute, crippled daughter of Mother Courage, takes a drum, climbs onto the stable roof, pulls up the ladder, and begins to pound the drum. The soldiers cannot reach the roof, so they shoot the girl and she falls. Meanwhile, however, her drumming has been heard in the town and has raised the alarm. Kattrin is dead, but the town is saved.

Don't pray; act! That is the incendiary summary of this eleventh scene. Prayer is flight from reality and from individual responsibility. Brecht staged that maxim most impressively. Of course, it does not occur to him that God could have acted through Kattrin. That is, if we take Brecht at his word Kattrin is driven to act precisely through the helpless prayer of her mother and the peasants.

## God's power in history

Rousseau, Kant, and Brecht have been influential. Their objections to petitionary prayer have fixed themselves in the heads of quite a few theologians who battle with the idea of petition, try to justify it, even to turn it into something they think justified, often in the process giving it a sense that makes petitionary prayer a mere camouflage for something else.

Ultimately the question is always: does God intervene in the course of world affairs? Does God even want to? Is that something worthy of God? Can such a thing be, in a world that is God's creation and has its own integrity?

This last question—let me call it, for now, the question of God's power in history—affects not only the question of petitionary prayer; it touches prayers of praise and thanksgiving also, because these are aroused not only by the beauty of creation. That is only a particular sector of biblical praise. What invites praise and thanksgiving in the

---

4. Translated to reflect the original dialect-flavored text, based on Bertolt Brecht, *Mother Courage and Her Children: A Chronicle of the Thirty Years' War*, English version by Eric Bentley (New York: Grove Press, 1955), 105–6, alt. LMM.

Bible is above all God's deeds in history. But if God does not act in the People of God, if God does not intervene, there is no basis on which the People of God should send up praise.

The question of God's power in history is thus one of the fundamental issues in all prayer—certainly the prayer of Jews and Christians. And it is obviously not only a question of whether God acted in the past, in biblical times. It is just as much about whether God acts in our days, in these present years. The question of God's power in history is the point of origin for most problems about prayer that irritate people today. For all these reasons I will pursue the question right away and not later in the chapter about prayers of petition.

## A basic biblical experience

Both the Old and the New Testaments tell us in many places that God is active in everything, that God guides history and even intervenes when Israel calls out to him. It really doesn't make much sense to quote individual texts on this point, since for the Bible that is simply a matter of course. There God's power in history is like a continuous basic melody that sustains everything; it is like a *cantus firmus*, embroidered with a variety of motifs but coming through again and again. The book of Isaiah has this divine self-description: "I form light and create darkness, I make weal and create woe; I the LORD do all these things" (Isa 45:7). That text presses against the boundary of what is theologically possible. It is intended to reject the activities of foreign gods and powers, so it has God creating not only weal but woe. But it is precisely in doing so that it speaks of God's sovereign creative and historical authority and power.

In the Old Testament the archetype of all divine action in history is Israel's exodus from Egypt, which is the great work of God in the midst of history. It is a miracle of pure grace. In the exodus God takes the initiative again and again. It is not Israel that fights against the Egyptians; God fights for Israel.

That is depicted in exemplary fashion in Exodus 14:13-14. The Israelites have arrived at the Sea of Reeds but have not yet crossed over. They are forming groups for the passage, but that puts them in a highly precarious situation and at that very moment the Egyptian chariots appear on the horizon.

> But Moses said to the people, "Do not be afraid, stand firm, and see the deliverance that the LORD will accomplish for you today; for the Egyptians whom you see today you shall never see again. The LORD will fight for you, and you have only to keep still."

Again the text presses against the limits of what is possible: Israel can put its hands in its lap and watch God acting. All it has to do is trust and stop trembling. It cannot be said more clearly by the use of narrative means: God intervenes in history.

But biblical faith in God's power in history achieves its absolute culmination in the New Testament confession "God raised Jesus from the dead," because God's raising of Jesus indeed means new creation beyond our earthly world—but new creation *not* isolated from history; rather, one that is a transformation of history itself brought about by creative power.

God transforms history that has happened and is happening into its ultimate meaning. It is the *crucified* Jesus who is raised. Raising Jesus from the dead is God's definitive demonstration that this God is the one God who always existed in biblical faith: the one who acts in the world, the God who is the absolute master of history. There is no need here for further citations and proofs.

To separate this faith from the Bible is to strike at its innermost self and to destroy the biblical texts. Then history would no longer be the interweaving of divine and human freedom; it would be something to which God has never laid claim and a sphere that was never subject to God's claim. Let me emphasize again: it would be absurd to suppose that God acted in God's people and the world in biblical times but then concluded the work and ceased to act. God either acts continually in the world or not at all.

Still, wasn't Jesus' resurrection the last, comprehensive, and concluding act of God, allowing for no new beginning of divine action? That is quite true—but we must immediately add that God's deeds also continue after Easter in that the definitive eschatological act of raising Jesus is manifested and developed in the midst of history as a church-creating act. In that sense God's historical actions continue beyond Easter and to the ends of the earth as powerful actions that we may confidently affirm as continuing to unfold and develop the Easter event.

## The world's autonomy

When all that is said we must, of course, add that God does not intervene in the course of the world by undermining the world's autonomy. Most certainly God does not act in history in defiance of human freedom. God does not tear a hole in physical chains of causality, and God does not impose divine freedom in place of human freedom. God does not ignore or defy God's own creation. In other words: God does not act as does an *earthly* cause, but in a way that corresponds to divine nature. God acts as a cause beyond and outside the world that sustains everything, effects all that is good, guides everything toward its goal, all without eliminating human free action.

So it is not without some danger that we speak of God's "intervention." After all, "intervention" means bringing a chain of events to a stop, setting switches, changing a program, falling into someone's arms, initiating things, starting developments, bringing new factors into play. That is how we speak of physical causes as well as of human actions and reactions. But that is *not* how God acts in the world. In that case God would be part of the universe, a cosmic energy or a force within history: in short, then God would no longer be God, but world.

## Contrary to all human doing

So when we speak about God's acting we can no longer make a positive image of it in our heads. We can speak of it only through images and analogies. We have to say that God acts—woe to us if we keep silent about it!—and yet we dare not speak of that acting as if it took place the way human action does. To use an image: God's action is transverse to all human action and to every chain of physical causality.

Something similar is true of Jesus Christ. Jesus is the absolute arrival of God in history. In him God has become personally present in the world. Jesus is truly human and truly divine, but we cannot form a positive idea of how the two go together. For example, we have no way of describing *how* human and divine consciousness fit together in Jesus.

What Jesus' disciples could see was a human being—certainly a human being who frightened and fascinated them; certainly a human being who spoke and acted "with authority." And yet there was no getting a handle on his divinity. The disciples could only perceive in faith that here God was acting in person. Here God has become ultimate presence. That was a genuine perception, and to that extent it is inappropriate to say "only." But it was a perception *in faith*.

The same is true, indeed, of every action of God in the world. We can neither analyze nor picture for ourselves how divine and human freedom subsist together: indeed, we cannot do so *in principle*. We can only look at history through the eyes of faith and say: here God acted. Here again, of course, "only" is inappropriate. Perception in faith is real perception, but not in accordance with the objectivizing methods of the sciences. Historians can affirm historical facts. That God is hidden behind those facts is something only faith can discern. God's "incognito" remains intact.

## A degree of modesty

All this has consequences for how we can speak of God's intervention in the world. Somehow or other our speaking in such matters must retain a certain modesty. We must not speak of God's action as if we can see it as clear as day. Here the Bible itself points us in the right direction. For example, in the story of David's ascent to the throne in 2 Samuel 10–20 and 1 Kings 1–2 the narrative sequence, with literary mastery, distinguishes between the independent course of history brought about by human beings and the working of God that lies behind all history.

The material of 2 Samuel 11 is trivial in itself: David, the great king of Israel, destroys the marriage of his officer, Uriah. While Uriah is fighting under General Joab against the Ammonites,

David takes his wife, Bathsheba, to bed. Bathsheba becomes pregnant, and her pregnancy must be concealed; hence the king tries every trick in the book to get Uriah to sleep with his wife during a leave at home. Because Uriah, a clever officer, sees through the plan of his supreme commander and does not fall in with it, he has to be gotten rid of—and so that he can be disposed of without notice, a number of other soldiers have to die with him.

There is great narrative skill in the way all that is told, with sober statement, psychological precision, and self-critical direct moral judgment. The story shows how one thing leads to another. David's lust in the beginning leads in the end to the murder of his own subordinates. Once having begun, David falls into a morass that draws him in deeper and deeper.

And where is God in all that? God in no way intervenes in the events. It seems as if God is altogether absent from the story. The whole thing is told as if God were not present at all. Only at the end of the long narrative in chapter 11 comes—suddenly and without preparation and therefore all the more effectively—the simple statement: "But the thing that David had done displeased the LORD" (2 Sam 11:27).

At that point God does, in fact, intervene. But how? God sends the prophet Nathan to David. So here again God does not act directly; God sends a prophet. We could also say that it becomes clear to Nathan that he dare not keep silent about the whole sequence of events, which of course was talked about surreptitiously in the royal court. So that is how God acts in 2 Samuel 11–12: not in the foreground. The story of God's intervention is narrated in the most tactful and reticent way imaginable. The same is true as the story of the royal succession proceeds.

## An assassination attempt

On May 13, 1981, the Turkish right-wing extremist Mehmet Ali Ağca attempted to assassinate Pope John Paul II in St. Peter's Square in Rome. The pope was severely wounded, taking three bullets. He attributed his survival to Mary and later interpreted the event by saying: "It was a mother's hand that guided the bullet's path and allowed the pope, who was struggling with death, to stop at its threshold." We would certainly not take such a statement literally. It reveals the vital, concrete faith of that great pope. Besides, his words reflect the way the Bible also speaks. For example, the Exodus narrative says that God clogged the wheels of the Egyptians' chariots so that they could scarcely move (Exod 14:25). Of course, for the most part the Bible sets up barriers to prevent the text's being misunderstood or it uses type-narratives that allow for such expressions. I don't find that kind of barrier in the pope's statement. He even moves, without noticing it, into a neighborhood that is not altogether appropriate in this instance.

I am referring to a passage in the *Iliad* that is strangely similar to John Paul II's image. The goddess Athena has persuaded one of the best archers in Troy to shoot at the Greek Menelaus, who is besieging Troy together with other kings and the gigantic Greek army. There is a lull in the fighting; the Greeks have no real desire to go on. The Trojan shoots accurately and would have killed Menelaus if Athena had not deflected the arrow:

> But you, Menelaus, the blessed deathless gods did not forget you,
> Zeus's daughter the queen of fighters first of all.
> She reared before you, skewed the tearing shaft,
> flicking it off your skin as quick as a mother
> flicks a fly from her baby sleeping softly.[5]

There follows a full description of how the goddess deflects the shaft to a part of the body where it tears a deep, horribly bleeding flesh wound, yet Menelaus's life is spared. The result of Athena's skillful trick is that the attack on Troy flares up again.

It may be that the astonishing resemblance of the pope's language to that of Homer should be a warning to us. Ought we to imagine God's working—in this case Mary's protection—as if we could perceive God's motives and ways of acting in detail in a this-worldly event? Nonbelievers can all too easily misunderstand that kind of talk. They can say: "If Mary had shifted the course

---

5. *The Iliad*, trans. Robert Fagles (New York: Viking Penguin, 1990), IV, ll. 127-31.

of the bullet a few centimeters the other way . . . why not shove it a little farther? Then the pope wouldn't have been hit at all."

## The cardinal and the gardener

There is an anecdote that warns us against saying the wrong thing about providence. Though it is not immediately obvious, the story is deeply theological:

> The French curial cardinal Eugène Tisserant often strolled through a Roman park where he frequently saw a gardener, always hard at work. One day the cardinal wanted to compliment the gardener and said to him: "The park is becoming more and more beautiful. It's obvious what can be achieved when human toil and divine providence work together." "You are right, Your Eminence," said the gardener. "You should have seen this park when nothing but providence was working on it."

Of course God was at work in the park, just as the whole world is God's work, but the cardinal's speech at least skirted the danger of praising an awkward model of cooperation: God does half and the human being does the other half. But in the case of an act of God with which humans cooperate the correct theological formula can only be that the human being must do everything without stinting (otherwise, in this case, there would be no park at all), and God must also do everything, nothing left out, although in God's own way and on a completely different level. The gardener was the better theologian of the two: he unmasked a false image of providence.

## A theory of petition

At the same time our reticence about speaking too superficially about God's acting should not lead us to see divine action as happening only through human action. There are some current theories about petitionary prayer that do exactly that. They go something like this:

Do my petitions change God and make God interfere in the ways of the world? No, my prayers only change me so that God can intervene in the world through me.   *transformative Prayer*

There is an element of truth in this and similar theories. Obviously an honest petition will change me—and that is true not only of petitions. Every prayer changes the one who prays. But if the only purpose of the prayer is to change me, its basic movement is twisted. Then prayer is no longer addressed to God but to my-self—not, of course, as self-worship, but as an impulse to a change of consciousness. Then God would only be a fake audience; the real one would be me. Prayer would ultimately become nothing more than a dialogue with myself and the story of two freedoms would become just the isolated story of an ego far away from God and reliant only on itself.

The dismissive theory of petition thus described can also appear in a softened variant: that the human being is the real, and indeed the only, gate through which God's action can enter the world. If God acts in the world it is only through people—because God can change the human heart through the Spirit, who kindles there the fire of God's love.

Obviously it is correct to say that God acts through people and that God gives them the divine Spirit. God acted in the world through Abraham, Moses, and the prophets, and the definitive, unsurpassable action of God in the world took place through Jesus Christ. God's power in history consists also in the fact that God again and again finds people who want nothing other than to do God's will.

Still, our view would be too narrow if we were to suppose that God is acting only where human conversion makes it possible for God's saving will to be realized. It is common today to hear more and more petitions based on precisely this way of thinking. So, for example, instead of praying, "Bring peace to the world," we say, "Guide the hearts of those in authority so that they will seek peace throughout the world." Apart from the fact that the authorities have only limited opportunities to seek peace, the causes of hatred and conflict in the world are much too complicated and hidden to be eliminated by purely political means. But that is not the point.

Much more serious is that petitions of this sort inevitably create the impression that God can only intervene in the world through human hearts.

Those who think that way not only diminish God's omnipotence but betray an odd idea of the world. Such prayers insinuate that God can indeed reach into human heads, but nowhere else. In reality it is just as true, obviously, of the human heart and brain as of other things in this world: God does not intervene directly anywhere. God does not interrupt any physical chains of causality; God's acting is crossways to every kind of this-worldly cause.

Besides, we must ask: what can human conversion achieve? Only the insight that grows in one's head? Or aren't there also external events that bring about insight? What about an illness, an accident, a web of "worldly" things that we cannot penetrate? For there is not only the action of God in humans and in history: beyond all that is God's universal activity, continually creating, sustaining, and maintaining the world—and not only that, but also bringing it toward its goal.

## God all in all

*Human* history is only a part of this all-encompassing movement. God effects all things everywhere, and the prayers of the People of God praise not only God's actions in history but also God's working in the universe. Paul concludes his reflections in Romans 11:33-36 on Israel's lack of faith and how God has acted throughout history even and especially through that unbelief with a hymn:

> O the depth of the riches and wisdom and knowledge of God!
> How unsearchable are his judgments and how inscrutable his
> ways!
> "For who has known the mind of the Lord?
>    Or who has been his counselor?"
> "Or who has given a gift to him,
>    to receive a gift in return?"
> For from him and through him and to him are all things. To him
> be the glory forever. Amen.

It may be that Paul himself was somewhat shocked by how thoroughly he had previously rendered the story of God's actions concrete. With this hymn he establishes a counterweight. In all the reflections that follow we should keep in mind the theology behind this song of praise. How the cooperation of God's freedom and our own takes place, how God's saving will and our prayers work together: all this is for us ultimately "unsearchable" and "inscrutable."

## Chapter 3

# The Church Has Many Forms of Prayer

In the first chapter we spoke of the basic direction of prayer: in the Holy Spirit through Christ to the Father. Ultimately it was about prayer as being drawn into the eternal conversation of the triune God. The Holy Spirit prays in us, those sanctified in baptism. The second chapter was about God's power in history: God acts in the world, but in a way incommensurable with all earthly chains of causality. This means that it takes place in a completely different dimension, and it is incalculable. If we want to approach what prayer really is, however, we have to pay attention to something else—and that is what this third chapter is about. Our prayer can take on the greatest variety of forms.

We begin simply with the word "prayer." It is a short word, elegantly shaped, immediately comprehensible to everyone. But it does not derive, as one might suppose, from the verb "to pray." Rather, it comes from "to ask." Originally it referred to the act of requesting. Evidently when the word "pray" was created people regarded asking as the primal form of prayer, but in the meantime it has become a general term. "Prayer" is the collective name for a whole variety of forms.

## As varied as life itself

Many Christians, it seems, are not at all aware that there are various forms of prayer. They have never thought about it. If you say to them, "There are petition, lament, thanksgiving, praise, adoration," they are astonished at first, but then they nod and say, "Of course there is a difference between 'asking' and 'thanking.' But I never heard that 'lamenting' can be a prayer."

In this book we will speak of a great variety of prayer forms—or, we might say, a variety of purposes for speaking, each of which produces different forms of prayer. First we will discuss praise, then petition, then lament as a forgotten but indispensable form of prayer, and finally meditation, which today has taken the place of prayer for many people who are no longer able to believe. Besides these we will speak of the Psalms and of the revolution taking place in Psalms scholarship; of so-called "imprecatory psalms"; of hymns; of the Eucharistic Prayer, the central locus of all Christian prayer; and finally of a very personal prayer history.

But why the distinctions? Isn't prayer simply prayer? Isn't it a kind of obsession on the part of scholars, this attempt to separate things into smaller and smaller categories? Doesn't that peculiar species, "scholars," have a kind of rage for classification in its genes that is not of the slightest use for daily living?

## Pure forms?

What a rampage Old Testament scholars went on in Psalms exegesis in past decades (more precisely since Hermann Gunkel [1862–1932]), dividing them into more and more difficult genres! They distinguish between individual songs of lament and group laments, between individual songs of thanksgiving and community thanksgivings, between individual songs of trust and community songs of trust, between hymns, royal psalms, songs of Zion, historical psalms, liturgies, and wisdom psalms. And in general that was correct.

The problem was only that in doing so they tried to reconstruct pure forms so far as possible. Whatever did not fit within the original form they themselves posited was rejected as secondary. The ideal of that generation of scholars was psalms that were constructed on the workbench, so to speak: psalms that met the ideals of Old Testament scholars to the last detail. That pure and unadulterated forms of speech are rare in real life, that many of the psalms display mixed forms, that speakers and attitudes could change within a psalm, and above all that great poets also experiment with forms and can use them for purposes different from the originals—none of that was really clear to the older generation of scholars.

Nevertheless, their questions about the genre of the Psalms were extremely fruitful because they help us to better understand the form, intent, and "life setting" (*Sitz im Leben*) of a psalm. And for that reason it is also important to speak in this book about the different forms of prayer. It makes a difference whether one praises God, thanks God, or asks God for something, whether one raises a lament before God, meditates, or adores in silence.

## Shifting stances and attitudes in prayer

Certainly in this regard we need to know that forms of prayer may shift very quickly within a single prayer situation. One may begin to implore God and find that passionate plea suddenly changing into a prayer of thanks. The petitioner has remembered, in the midst of pleading, how often God has already helped her and rescued her from crises.

Or: a prayer begins with wild protest against God and hideous lament—but as he goes on lamenting, the person praying becomes quieter and quieter, and suddenly his prayer is a hope-filled plea.

Or: someone begins to recite fixed, prescribed prayers, and suddenly she is overwhelmed and cannot utter another word of prayer because she senses that everything she is saying to God is inadequate. She wants to be wordless before God. She simply offers her heart to God, and this brimful silence before the face of God is pure happiness for her.

Praying cannot be any different from other parts of daily life. There too we experience swiftly changing attitudes and, consequently, different forms of speech. We need to be aware of how fast our way of speaking can change in any ordinary situation. No sooner have two people who know each other well offered greetings to each other than they begin to exchange information. Then one of them suddenly utters a loud complaint against politicians who seem to him completely useless. The other person asks him to calm down. The first one begins to defend his point of view, then apologizes, whereupon the other concedes that there really are some things in politics that are bitterly annoying. And so it goes on. The dialogue moves from one form of speech to another. For example, the series can be something like

Greeting

Exchange of information

Lament

Petition

Defense

Apology

Agreement

More information

More lamenting

Soothing

Wish

Parting

Obviously there are also phases in which the forms of speech mix and combine, and there may suddenly be a brief phase of silence in the midst of the conversation. How pleasant it is when a conversation comes to rest and that rest signals complete agreement!

## Instinctive knowledge

For the most part we don't even think about all this; we do it instinctively. We are certainly in a position to distinguish all sorts of speech forms. It is clear to us that a eulogy is something different from a sales pitch. We know that a weather report is not the same as a set of instructions for how to use something. We can separate news from commentary and a declaration of love from mere information.

Still, we don't always pay attention to these differences. For example, how embarrassing it would be if a declaration of love were confused with a lecture. Let's imagine the following situation: he (age eighteen) sits close to her (age seventeen) on a warm evening in May, on a bench near a lake. The nightingales are singing; the frogs are peeping. Then "he" (of course it is the man; no woman would talk this way) says:

> There is a lot in favor of the idea that I love you. Let me offer three reasons:
>
> (1) Your looks appeal to me. You have such lovely eyes, and your hair is of a splendid color.
>
> (2) I have noticed that I can talk with you easily, at least most of the time.
>
> (3) I think that for some time I have sensed signs from you that lead me to believe that you, too, have some feelings of affection toward me.
>
> In summary conclusion from those three points I may say, "I love you." Of course, with regard to this perhaps somewhat daring statement I must add some conditions.

And so on in the same fashion. Oh, heavens, is that ever embarrassing! You will certainly object that no such thing could happen, at least not nowadays. Attitudes have changed so much! I admit I have been exaggerating; the scene is imaginary. But how often, for example, does it happen that someone confuses the genre "table conversation" with that of "lecture." Good conversations at table should not turn into lectures; they should establish communication. They ought to be like the salt in the soup, giving extra flavor to the meal. Certainly they may convey information, but only in appropriate quantities. When somebody starts delivering a lecture or a long speech at table, it turns our stomachs.

All that is only meant to show that in everyday life there are the most varied forms of speech, and so it cannot be any different in the case of prayer. Therefore it makes a lot of sense to appreciate the special nature of the various forms of prayer. That itself will help us to deal with prayer in appropriate fashion and above all as "fitting the person concerned."

## Petitions in crisis

To take one example: a community gathered for worship is nowadays confronted quite often with petitions that are no longer appeals to God in the true sense but are something very different. For example, what should we make of the following petition, taken from one of the many books of prayers for church use now on the market:

> For the Christian churches:
> That they may show more understanding
> for the problems and difficulties
> with which people have to struggle today;
> that they do more than in the past
> to cooperate in improving the structures of society;
> that they recognize their responsibility
> for the future of humanity;
> and that all their teachings and norms
> may be truly a help, and not a burden, for humanity.
> For this we ask you to hear us.

What is that, really? Is it a little sermon for bishops and superintendents? Or is it a stylized vision for the gathered community of what the church should be? Or has someone just given vent to his or her frustration with the churches? In any case there is no escaping the suspicion that it is not God who is addressed here but, instead, the congregation that is forced to listen, or maybe just some imaginary audience.

Admittedly, it is no easy matter to write appropriate petitions. First one must know what petitions are: they are not statements of position camouflaged in prayer style; they are not theological instructions for the community; they are not substitute sermons;

they are not even laments about the state of the world and the church. They are appeals to God and pleas for God's help. Obviously the need must be named, but in such a way that it is clearly God who is addressed, and therefore one may assume that God knows what the prayer is about. There is no need for long explanations about the state of the world, and so the appeals need not be excessive. They can remain relatively brief.

It is in that regard especially that the ancient petitions and collects of the Roman Church furnish us with models. Consider, for example, the "Solemn Intercessions" of Good Friday, which retain a very early form of church petitions. The petition "for those in tribulation" reads:

> Let us pray, dearly beloved,
> to God the Father almighty,
> that he may cleanse the world of all errors,
> banish disease, drive out hunger,
> unlock prisons, loosen fetters,
> granting to travelers safety, to pilgrims return,
> health to the sick, and salvation to the dying.

This last of the "Solemn Intercessions" is rather long; after all, it is a summary petition. But the individual appeals are laconically succinct. "That he may . . . drive out hunger"—it couldn't be said more briefly. After all, God knows why there is hunger and how dreadful it is, and that we human beings share in the guilt for the fact that there are still so many hungry people in the world does not necessarily have to be spelled out in a petition. The homily would be the right place for that. The petition is addressed to God the Father: it is God who must act, because the need cries out to heaven. It is certainly true that we ourselves must also act, but that is not the subject of petitions, which are addressed to God, not to the community. So there is no need to say, for example:

> Banish hunger from the world
> by opening the eyes of us Christians
> to the suffering in the developing world,
> and change our hearts through your Spirit,
> that we ourselves may help those who are hungry.

That kind of urgent pedagogy can only get on the nerves of church-goers. The petition I have just quoted is couched in ugly language and—I repeat—it misnames the addressee(s). Here, then, we can learn a lot from the ancient Roman liturgy.

Besides, there is still another reason why the Solemn Interces-sions of Good Friday are so concisely formulated: after the state-ment of what is now to be prayed for, the deacon used to say or sing: "*Flectamus genua!*—Let us kneel." (In the newer Missals a pe-riod of silence is prescribed here.) Here is the place for individual prayer; formerly it ended with the command "*Levate!*—Arise." So, since there is sufficient space for individual silent prayer, the statement of the topic at the beginning can and must be brief. Likewise, the concluding collect can also be brief, summarizing the silent prayer of the people. In this case it reads:

> Almighty ever-living God,
> comfort of mourners, strength of all who toil,
> may the prayers of those who cry out in any tribulation
> come before you,
> that all may rejoice,
> because in their hour of need
> your mercy was at hand.
> Through Christ our Lord.

What is especially evident in the Good Friday orations applies to every Roman collect. It begins with the priest's "Let us pray," which should be followed by a long-enough pause for personal, individual prayer. Only then does the priest collect the personal prayers with a concluding formula. That is why the Roman collects are also so brief. They are indeed *Collecta*, collects, in their basic structure: the gathering-up of the prayers of the faithful.

## The Roman collects

At this point it is worthwhile to take a closer look at the structure of such collects. First all the people are called to pray; prayerful silence follows. Then comes the address to God; in the collect just cited it is "Almighty ever-living God." We already know that this address is not directed to God as a Trinity of persons but to God the Father alone. The salutation can, however, also be "Almighty God," or "God, our Father," or "Lord," or "Lord our God." Such phrases are familiar in the Roman Missal. In the Latin model the salutation is usually very brief: simply *"Deus"* (God) or *"Domine"* (Lord) or *"Omnipotens Deus"* (Almighty God) or at most *"Omnipotens sempiterne Deus"* (Almighty ever-living God).

The salutation is always followed by an expansion in the form of praise—a statement either of what God has done (narrative praise) or who God is (descriptive praise). In the collect cited above from the Solemn Intercessions for Good Friday the praise is descriptive: "comfort of mourners, strength of all who toil."

The praise is then followed by the petition itself, ordinarily in an artistic, highly rhetorical style that, however, is usually only recognizable as such in the original Latin. Only that version reveals how the prayer works with sounds, rhythms, figures of speech, and allusions to biblical texts.

The collect ends with a closing formula, either in the form of a solemn doxology or, as in this case, with the expression "[we ask this] through Christ our Lord." The congregation responds with "Amen," which means that it appropriates and affirms what the priest has summarized.

We see that the Roman collect is a very well-developed, securely shaped, consistently structured, and theologically considered form of prayer. It includes the congregation and even—assuming that the priest is not afraid of prayerful silence—accords it an essential place. It thus shows the seriousness of the fact that there must be periods of silence within the worship service, and the spoken elements are exemplary in their brevity. The Roman collect is a petition, but in the expansion of the salutation it is also confessional praise. We can learn especially from the collects in the Missal what a fixed, formal genre of speech is.

## Fundamentals

This chapter has tried to show that there are many different forms of prayer and to introduce the varieties of praise, thanksgiving, petition, lament, and adoration. But here at the end all that has to be relativized again to a certain degree. Ultimately, in the People of God every prayer is at depth more than praise, thanksgiving, petition, and lament. Let me demonstrate this on the basis of the Lord's Prayer.

In its external form the Our Father is pure petition. We have to see that first of all, because otherwise we may overlook the urgency and intensity of this prayer. The concluding praise— "For the kingdom, the power, and the glory are yours, now and for ever"—was attached to the Our Father at a later date. The oldest and best manuscripts do not yet contain that ending. In all probability it stems from a time when the Our Father became part of the eucharistic celebration. In any case a closing doxology for the Our Father is first attested in the *Didachē*, the *Teaching of the Twelve Apostles*, our oldest church order (ca. 120 CE). There it agrees in part with the closing doxologies of the eucharistic prayers collected in the *Didachē*. So originally the Our Father was pure petition.

Why didn't Jesus teach his disciples a prayer of praise as their very own—or at the very least a petition combined with praise? Why not a prayer similar to the *amidah*, the Jewish Eighteen Benedictions? The *amidah* begins:

> Blessed are you, O Lord our God and God of our fathers, the God of Abraham, the God of Isaac and the God of Jacob, the great, mighty and revered God, the Most High God who bestows lovingkindnesses, the creator of all things, who remembers the good deeds of the patriarchs and in love will bring a redeemer to their children's children for his name's sake. O king, helper, savior and shield. Blessed are you, O Lord, the shield of Abraham.

The reason why Jesus did not teach his disciples a prayer of praise was probably that the disciples, of course, prayed the usual Jewish prayers, and they certainly contained praise. But they wanted a specific prayer corresponding to their existence as disciples, and so Jesus taught them the Our Father. In every petition it reflects the special situation of Jesus and his disciples, their itinerant existence, and the need to proclaim the reign of God. At the same time it reflects the urgent need of the People of God. The Our Father is like a cry, a shout begging God to intervene.

That must be said. We dare not simply change the Our Father into a prayer of thanksgiving and praise as Albrecht Ritschl once did. But that is not the whole issue.

What happens, in fact, when someone wants to live as Jesus' disciple and thus slowly, without understanding what is happening within, moves ever deeper into "fundamental," "unknown" regions of prayer? Such a one increasingly understands that God is holy, that he himself is a sinner. Such a one becomes more and more aware that he may approach this holy God only with the greatest reverence, give his whole life into God's hands without any further reservation, that despite all guilt and undeserving, the Spirit of God dwells in him and that there is nothing more tragic than to grieve this Holy Spirit, the dearest and best guest in his life (Eph 4:30).

When one has experienced all that more and more deeply, and when she is touched by love of God, often very softly but like a profound happiness, all external forms of prayer draw closer and closer together. She still praises God—how could she not?—and yet she knows that no praises can completely comprehend God, who is infinitely greater than them all. She still thanks God—with a joyful heart—but she knows that all these relationships of thanksgiving are but fragmentary. She still asks God for many things—often in tears—but she continually enters phases where she would prefer not to ask for anything. She still laments her suffering before God—but in complete trust. After all, she has so often found her laments turning into joy.

All the external forms of prayer remain, but they are transformed from within into a kind of prayer that has no name. Such a one prays even the Our Father in a new way, being so certain that God will do everything asked in the Lord's Prayer (for example, that God will inevitably bring God's reign into being) that it is really no longer a prayer of petition. The types of prayer that had been so clearly distinct now dissolve into one another or vanish entirely. Now there is nothing to be done but to hold out one's heart to God, surrender oneself to God, and do God's will. Petition is transformed into adoration.

To make all that clear through another example: the *Kyrie eleison* at the beginning of the Mass was originally a cry for help. Its first meaning was "Lord, have mercy!" But, similarly to *Hosanna*, which really means "Save us!" it acquired the additional character of a cry of greeting, even a joyous call. When we sing or speak the *Kyrie* at the beginning of Mass we are greeting the Christ who enters among us. The character of petition is not lost, for petition, greeting, cry of jubilation all resonate together—and the resonance is still greater than that. Those who repeatedly recite a prayer—for example, the "Jesus prayer" ("Jesus, Son of David, have mercy on me")—will find the *Kyrie* the expression of their whole praying existence. It contains everything—the sum of suffering, hopes, expectations, trust, affection, surrender, adoration—in its very essence.

*Chapter 4*

# Praise Is for a Reason

## Comprehensive praise

Now let us turn to our first form of prayer: praise. To answer the question of what praise really is we will orient ourselves to Sacred Scripture and there undertake a close examination of Psalm 145. It bears the subtitle "Praise," in Hebrew *tehillah*. It is true that the superscriptions in the Psalter are not as old as the psalms themselves; they were added later. Still, Psalm 145 is the only one bearing the genre designation "Praise." Why was this psalm in particular given that designation? It was because of its frame, which begins:

> I will extol you, my God and King,
>    and bless your name forever and ever.
> Every day I will bless you,
>    and praise your name forever and ever. (Ps 145:1-2)

And the psalm ends with:

> My mouth will speak the praise of the Lord,
>    and all flesh will bless his holy name forever and ever.
>       (Ps 145:21)

But not only that! The whole psalm—not just the beginning and ending—is shot through with the vocabulary of praise. It never stops speaking of praising, lauding, proclaiming, making known, and exalting the LORD. It calls for the whole of human existence, indeed of the entire world, to become one single act of praise. Psalm 145 also expresses this all-encompassing demand by its alphabetic structure: each new verse begins with the next letter of the Hebrew alphabet. For people of that time the letters A to Z (in Hebrew Aleph to Tau) meant much more than they do to us today. They saw the alphabet as a miracle because it contained the whole of language and so the whole world. Of course, the artistic game with the alphabet that Psalm 145 exhibits cannot be reproduced in translation. But let us look more closely at the psalm itself, which, incidentally, influenced the *Te Deum*:

> ¹I will extol you, my God and King,
>     and bless your name forever and ever.
> ²Every day I will bless you,
>     and praise your name forever and ever.
> ³Great is the LORD, and greatly to be praised;
>     his greatness is unsearchable.
> ⁴One generation shall laud your works to another,
>     and shall declare your mighty acts.
> ⁵On the glorious splendor of your majesty,
>     and on your wondrous works, I will meditate.
> ⁶The might of your awesome deeds shall be proclaimed,
>     and I will declare your greatness.
> ⁷They shall celebrate the fame of your abundant goodness,
>     and shall sing aloud of your righteousness.
> ⁸The LORD is gracious and merciful,
>     slow to anger and abounding in steadfast love.
> ⁹The LORD is good to all,
>     and his compassion is over all that he has made.
> ¹⁰All your works shall give thanks to you, O LORD,
>     and all your faithful shall bless you.
> ¹¹They shall speak of the glory of your kingdom,
>     and tell of your power,
> ¹²to make known to all people your mighty deeds,
>     and the glorious splendor of your kingdom.
> ¹³Your kingdom is an everlasting kingdom,
>     and your dominion endures throughout all generations.
> The LORD is faithful in all his words,
>     and gracious in all his deeds.

<sup>14</sup>The LORD upholds all who are falling,
   and raises up all who are bowed down.
<sup>15</sup>The eyes of all look to you,
   and you give them their food in due season.
<sup>16</sup>You open your hand,
   satisfying the desire of every living thing.
<sup>17</sup>The LORD is just in all his ways,
   and kind in all his doings.
<sup>18</sup>The LORD is near to all who call on him,
   to all who call on him in truth.
<sup>19</sup>He fulfills the desire of all who fear him;
   he also hears their cry, and saves them.
<sup>20</sup>The LORD watches over all who love him,
   but all the wicked he will destroy.
<sup>21</sup>My mouth will speak the praise of the LORD,
   and all flesh will bless his holy name forever and ever.

## Arcs of suspense

If we examine the psalm more closely we notice a number of suspenseful arcs. It begins in the first person and ends the same way: "My mouth will speak the praise of the LORD." This "I" appears also in verses 5 and 6, but everywhere else the text speaks in the plural of those offering praise. The shift is especially abrupt in verse 6:

> The might of your awesome deeds shall be proclaimed,
>    and I will declare your greatness.

Here we encounter an important phenomenon that appears throughout the Psalter. The rapid shift from singular to plural (or the reverse) is found not only in Psalm 145; it happens in many psalms. It signals that the one praying is not just an isolated individual. Even when praying out of a horrible crisis that has just fallen upon *him*, this person is praying with the whole of Israel. Likewise, when an individual raises a song of praise because *she* has been moved by God's glory, she praises the LORD together with all Israel. The psalm-singer's "I" is complex; in most cases it is also the "I" of Israel and sometimes even the "I" of the nations.

Who, then, is to praise the LORD in Psalm 145? Obviously the individual who is praying, the "I" in the psalm. But according to verse 10 "all your faithful" are also to give praise—that is, all Israel or a large group within Israel. And the arc extends still further. According to verse 21 "all flesh"—that is, every living thing—is to offer praise: all people and even all the animals.

This is to say that we have to consider that Psalm 145 does not stand in isolation; it is a transition to the last part of the whole Psalter, Psalms 146–150, the so-called "Final Hallel." Each of those psalms begins and ends with "Hallelujah," that is, "Praise YAH" (= "Praise YHWH"). The last five psalms are a single song of praise to God—praise that goes forth from Zion and in which the whole creation joins: sun and moon, fire and hail, snow and mist, mountains and hills, the wild beasts and all domestic animals, the kings of the earth and, finally, all nations (cp. Ps 148).

The Final Hallel of the Psalter is like a grand finale accompanied by a whole band of instruments (cp. Ps 150) and sung by the choir of the universe. This finale is to be read eschatologically: at the end of history the whole world will be pure praise. Those who pray the book of 150 psalms, ascending from dismal lament and urgent petition to culminate in the sounding praise of the whole creation, already anticipate the eternal finale of creation and history; indeed, they help it to begin already. Psalm 145 prepares for this final orchestration of Psalms 146–150: it is the symphonic transition. When Psalm 145 concludes "all flesh will bless his holy name forever and ever" we already hear the first notes of the Final Hallel of the Psalter with its intermingling of Israel, the world of the nations, and the universe.

The arcs of tension in Psalm 145 also include the so-called "shifting direction of speech." What is that? In verses 1 and 2 God is praised in direct address, but in verse 3 God is referred to in the third person: "Great is the LORD, and greatly to be praised." Then the text proceeds in "thou style," that is, as direct address to God. This strange shift from "thou" to "he" occurs repeatedly in our psalm. What are we to think of that?

In part the shifts are explained by the content. Psalm 145 draws its material from the whole Bible; it quotes, refers, engages in wordplay. Verse 8, for example ("The LORD is gracious and merciful, slow to anger and abounding in steadfast love"), quotes Exodus 34:6, the so-called "graciousness formula." It is in the third person in Exodus and therefore is quoted in the same style in our psalm. This necessitates disrupting the second-person style in verses 7 and 10.

But such observations are more a matter for specialists. What interests us here is something different. When we speak of God in the third person we start out in the speech-attitude of "confession." Our confession of faith, for example, is formulated entirely in the third person. It is directed not to God but to human beings before whom the speakers of the Credo publicly declare their faith. When God is praised in the third person—something that happens in the Psalter not only here but in many other places as well—a theological statement is made: no one can praise God without communicating that praise to others or joining with others in expressing praise. But when we join with others and call out to them how great God is, that confessional calling-out-to-one-another is nothing other than praise.

We can see that very clearly in a text that plays an important role within the Eucharistic Prayer, namely, the *Sanctus*. The first part takes up a heavenly liturgy as described by the prophet Isaiah in his call-vision. Seraphim stand about the throne of God and call to one another:

> Holy, holy, holy is the Lord of hosts;
> The whole earth is full of his glory. (Isa 6:3)

In its external form, as presented by Isaiah, that is certainly a confession of faith. The seraphim do not address God but cry out their "Holy, holy" to one another. But in reality it is altogether praise and adoration. The third-person style does not change that in the least. Confession and praise melt into one another. We can see that very beautifully expressed as the *Sanctus* continues with the *Hosanna* that the crowds shouted to each other when Jesus entered Jerusalem:

> Hosanna in the highest.
> Blessed is he who comes in the name of the Lord.
> Hosanna in the highest. (cp. Matt 21:9)

Thus the third person is in itself a mutual exchange. In reality it is praise of Jesus, who now enters in the name of God. Confession and praise have long since fused.

So we come to the third arc of tension in Psalm 145, the one that is crucial for us. We may ask quite simply: what is it for which God is actually being praised? Our psalm is not the least bit shy about that. It speaks of the greatness of the Lord, the brilliance of the Lord's majesty, goodness, justice—and affirms that the Lord is gracious and merciful, slow to anger and rich in steadfast love. Above all, in its middle section Psalm 145 speaks of the "glory of his kingdom." The abstract term *malkuth* ("kingship," "royal rule," "royal realm") appears no fewer than four times in verses 11-13. It is the same word Jesus uses when he speaks of the "reign [or: kingdom] of God."

As we have said, Psalm 145 is not shy about describing the greatness and majesty of God, the Lord and King. The first part of the psalm (vv. 2-13) is especially full of this "descriptive praise." But it is important that the psalm does not stop there. If it did, there would be something indeterminate about the psalm. We would not be sure of the reason or occasion for it. How does it happen that people take it upon themselves, in the first place, to speak of God's royal rule, God's majesty and justice?

The answer is found in the second part of the psalm (vv. 14-20). The first part certainly speaks of God's "works" and "mighty acts," "awesome deeds" and "wondrous works," but it all remains abstract. It is only in its second part that the psalm becomes concrete:

> The LORD upholds all who are falling (v. 14)
>    and raises up all who are bowed down (v. 14).
> . . . give[s] them their food in due season (v. 15)
> . . . satisfying the desire of every living thing (v. 16).
> [The LORD] fulfills the desire of all who fear him (v. 19);
>    . . . hears their cry, and saves them (v. 19).
> The LORD watches over all who love him (v. 20),
>    . . . all the wicked he will destroy (v. 20).

Verbs about God's actions pile upon themselves here. "Descriptive praise" becomes "reporting praise." It is evidently not enough just to speak of God's majesty and glory; it is necessary to show how that glory can be experienced. That is the precise reason why we encounter reporting praise at so many places in the Psalter. What God has done must be proclaimed. That fact will confront us with some very critical questions at the end of this chapter.

## A consequential "for"

Psalm 145's genre is that of the hymn. Within that genre there is a special form in which the causal connection between God's deeds in history and the praise they evoke is much more clearly stated than in Psalm 145. We can take Psalm 98 as one example:

> O sing to the LORD a new song,
>> *for* he has done marvelous things.
> His right hand and his holy arm
>> have gotten him victory.
> The LORD has made known his victory;
>> he has revealed his vindication in the sight of the nations.
> He has remembered his steadfast love and faithfulness
>> to the house of Israel.
>> All the ends of the earth have seen
>> the victory of our God. (Ps 98:1-3)

"O sing to the LORD a new song" is clearly the introduction. It is a call to praise God. Why a "new song"? Not because the old ones are worn out, used up, or have become boring. No, something new has happened, namely, "marvelous things" wrought by God, and the new thing calls for new songs. This makes it clear that it is *Israel* that is to sing the new songs, but in verses 4-6 the call goes out to all nations, and verses 7-9 will even summon the whole of Nature to sing with joy. And that is only the introduction!

The hymn itself begins by reciting God's new acts and, like many others of the same genre, it is introduced by "for" (Hebrew *ki*, Greek *hoti*). So praising God is not just accidental or self-motivated; there are reasons for it. What is that reason in our psalm? What does the singer mean, in this case, by God's marvelous deeds?

"His right hand and his holy arm have gotten him victory." With this the singer reveals an inevitable association with the Exodus (cp. Exod 15:6, 12, 16). But since "all the ends of the earth have seen the victory of our God" clearly alludes to the theology of Deutero-Isaiah (cp. Isa 52:10), the subject here must be the second exodus, that is, the return of the deported from Babylon. Naturally this elevates to the universal level an event that at the time would certainly not have been perceived by all nations, but that is something that can indeed occur as part of a song of praise. The singer sees in limited and often merely regional events a portent of future happenings with the same or similar structure. Indeed, because the singer sees the God who is master of history at work, for her or him God's present acts are already the beginning of the all-encompassing eschatological action that will embrace the world of the nations and the whole universe.

## Praise on the lips of Jesus

There are many other hymns in the Psalter and outside it (cp., for example, Sir 51:1-12) in which we encounter the word "for," introducing the reason for this particular praise. Do we find this theologically weighty "for" in the New Testament also?

The gospels contain many scenes in which Jesus is praying. Matthew 11:25-27 depicts him uttering praise:

> I thank you, Father, Lord of heaven and earth, *because* [*hoti*] you have hidden these things from the wise and the intelligent and have revealed them to infants; yes, Father, for such was your gracious will. All things have been handed over to me by my Father; and no one knows the Son except the Father, and no one knows the Father except the Son and anyone to whom the Son chooses to reveal him.

First of all let me say that in what follows I will not be considering whether this prayer comes from Jesus himself, nor will I ask about the historical situation in which it might have originated. Those are not the questions that interest me here. I am concerned only with the text as it stands. It is quite clearly a prayer of praise with an opening matching the generic style and, immediately after that, a reason for the praise, introduced in Greek by *hoti* (= "because," "for").

We have already seen that every praise of God is always already a confession, a creedal statement, and that every confession of God can easily turn into praise. That exactly matches the verb with which our text begins. In Greek it is *exhomologoumai*, which means both "I confess" and "I praise." But what causes Jesus to confess and praise his Father in heaven? The text gives three reasons:

First there is a more or less *formal* reason: God has hidden things from the wise and intelligent and has revealed them to "infants." That was God's pleasure, God's desire, God's joy. God is most attached to the "little" people, the despised. This is said without any animosity toward the wise. It is simply what it is. And the fact that it is what it is causes Jesus' praise to break forth.

But what are the "things" that God has revealed to the little and the despised? Here we arrive at the *substantive* reason for the praise that breaks forth from Jesus. The reason is named in what follows immediately: the Father has handed himself over completely to the Son, placing "everything" in his hands. Thus Jesus now, in person, is the unreserved communication of the Father. That it is especially the little ones and the infants who understand this secret that Jesus knows: that is why Jesus praises the Father.

But Jesus' cry of joy also has an *external* reason, an occasion: Matthew 11:25-27 is immediately preceded by a scene in which Jesus turns with harsh words of judgment toward Chorazin, Bethsaida, and Capernaum. In spite of all the miracles he has performed in those cities there is no conversion there. Matthew links Jesus' words of woe over those towns with his shout of praise. Apparently the wise and intelligent are to be found wherever—as in Chorazin, Bethsaida, and Capernaum—people remain indifferent to Jesus, and evidently the miracle that, in spite of such indifference, Jesus has found disciples among the little and despised is the reason why he praises the Father. That is how Matthew sees it, at any rate. He even links the scenes by how he presents them, joining the two passages with *apokritheis* ("he continued").

Thus even Jesus' praise does not arise simply from admiration of God's greatness and glory. It is evoked by a real situation: Jesus reacts to the indifference he encounters. It is only in the face of that indifference that he grasps the extent of the little people's faith, and so he praises the Father because it is precisely these "infants"—these unlettered ones—who are aware of the mystery.

## A revolutionary song

The fourth text I will treat in this chapter is the *Magnificat* (Luke 1:46-55). The same is true of this passage as of Jesus' exultant shout: we are not interested in historical examination but simply in the theological interpretation. Which is the prayer genre of the *Magnificat*? We could also ask: what kind of psalm does Mary sing? The answer is clear: this is a hymn. The *Magnificat* has an introduction characteristic of a hymn:

> ⁴⁶My soul magnifies the Lord,
> ⁴⁷and my spirit rejoices in God, my Savior.

This introduction is followed, in correct form, by the reason for praise, introduced by the now-familiar "for," which is in fact doubled here:

> ⁴⁸*for* he has looked with favor on the lowliness of his servant.
>     Surely, from now on all generations will call me blessed;
> ⁴⁹*for* the Mighty One has done great things for me,
>     and holy is his name.
> ⁵⁰His mercy is for those who fear him
>     from generation to generation.

All that refers to God's action in Mary. Then follow seven statements reporting God's other deeds:

> ⁵¹He has shown strength with his arm;
>     he has scattered the proud in the thoughts of their hearts.
> ⁵²He has brought down the powerful from their thrones,
>     and lifted up the lowly;
> ⁵³he has filled the hungry with good things,
>     and sent the rich away empty.
> ⁵⁴He has helped his servant Israel,
>     in remembrance of his mercy,
> ⁵⁵according to the promise he made to our ancestors,
>     to Abraham and to his descendants forever.

From beginning to end of her hymn Mary speaks of things that have already happened: what God has done in her and what God has done in Israel. The two are most intimately connected. The conception announced by the angel is not a private matter for Mary; it exceeds all the expectations, desires, and hopes that parents normally invest in their child. This conception places Mary in the space of God's acting since Abraham—that is, in a sphere in which all merely human desire is far surpassed. In that sense there is no discrepancy at all between the action of God in Mary and God's past action in Israel. But what are the concrete references of verses 51-54?

These verses constitute a mosaic of allusions to the Old Testament. For Jewish Christians it was clear what events were in view; they knew their Bible better than we do. "He has shown strength with his arm" alludes to the destruction of the Egyptians at the Sea of Reeds and thus to the whole story of Israel's being led out of Egypt. "He has filled the hungry with good things" points to the people's being fed with manna in the wilderness, and "he has helped his servant Israel" refers primarily to Israel's being brought back from Babylon, for the choice of words draws on the text of Isaiah 41:8-9.

But we may not only ask what is being referred to in the *Magnificat* at this and that point. We must also see what *kind* of event is being described here. When the mighty are brought down from their thrones, when they are chased out of their centers of power and scattered, when the rich suddenly stand with empty hands (let's say "with empty bank accounts") while the little and the lowly are made rich and their stomachs are finally filled—that is nothing other than revolution, overthrow, and the reversal of all social relationships.

So the *Magnificat* is by no means innocuous. It is a revolutionary anthem. Words like these—that the mighty are being cast down from their thrones and the poor and despised are being raised up—are otherwise to be heard only on the lips of revolutionaries. Mary is really singing about a revolution that turns everything upside down. It began with Abraham. It happened when Israel revolted against Pharaoh and his theocracy. It happened again and again when Israel listened to God and opened its actions to God. That revolution has now culminated in Mary and her messianic child.

No indeed, that is no gentle, mild song. Mary holds nothing back; she speaks in plain language. It is only our pious familiarity with the text that makes us ignore the Marseillaise-like keenness of the *Magnificat*. It by no means advocates being puny or unassuming. It praises the God of Israel who helps the despised to achieve their rights and shows the pompous and arrogant their proper place.

The location of this revolution is Israel; it is the church; it is our communities. Or we may say more precisely: that is where it should be, at any event, when these sing the *Magnificat* and don't let it be just empty words. The church should be that place in the world where the new society begins, the one about which the *Magnificat* and Jesus' Beatitudes speak: the place where the hungry are filled, the oppressed receive their just due, and there is an end to the weeping of the poor.

## Praise as we currently experience it

But that was a digression, intended to prevent us from ignoring the explosive power of the *Magnificat*. In this chapter on praise there is something else equally important, and that is what I want to emphasize here: readers will long since have wondered why I repeatedly stress so pointedly that biblical praise always has a historical context that evokes it. My stubborn insistence is based on the experience that our praise—and indeed, its liturgical form in particular—is often dry and bloodless. It doesn't flow. It doesn't come from the heart. It doesn't proceed from some deep place. Worship services, all too often, are mere obligatory ceremonies or a habit one doesn't (yet) want to give up. The next generation will do it. Where does that come from?

Obviously there are many reasons, but one of them is that liturgical praise lacks a basis. It needs to arise out of real experience: God has helped; God has acted; God has intervened; God has become our rescuer. But where do our congregations ever experience such a thing? Are there assemblies and worship services in which God's deeds *today* are told?

We read, in our assemblies, about the works of God. Notice: I say *read*, not *tell*. We read about deeds of God that happened in a long-ago time. It is right to do so; those past events are the basis of everything we are and do. But if we no longer experience a *present* action of God in us and in God's people we cannot have a clear picture of God's *previous* actions. In fact, they become unbelievable.

It would be instructive to study the church's history for the sole purpose of discovering the degree to which, in different centuries, people had experiences of salvation and openly proclaimed them. It is clear that they had their place in the realm of "private" devotion. We only need think of the countless pilgrimage sites and the votive plaques that hang there. For centuries pilgrimage sites have been indicators of the inextinguishable human longing to experience a living church. Such a church involves getting on the road, locking up our houses, leaving our elders behind, appealing to God in physical and spiritual crisis, confessing our guilt, finding help—and giving public testimony to that help. That is just what happened and still happens in many pilgrimage sites.

But do these basic Christian experiences take place in the everyday life of our congregations as well? If so, are they reflected on? Do parishes have any kind of institutional framework for speaking about the current actions of God in the world church, in the diocese, and in the individual parish—with biblical candor and without embarrassment? Those who assert that such a thing is impossible *in principle* because it is sectarian or deviant are refuted by the Acts of the Apostles.

## Telling the works of God

The Acts of the Apostles, in fact, gives evidence that in the early church there were frequent worship assemblies at which people reported how God had acted. For example, when Paul and Barnabas returned from their so-called first missionary journey, having been solemnly dispatched by the community at Antioch (see Acts 13:2-4), the author of Acts describes their return as follows:

> From there [Attalia] they sailed back to Antioch, where they had been commended to the grace of God for the work that they had completed. When they arrived, they called the church together and related all that God had done with them, and how he had opened a door of faith for the Gentiles. (Acts 14:26-27)

This text follows a pattern that occurs a number of times in Acts:

1. Arrival or return of community members (4:23; 12:16; 14:26; 15:4)

2. Then: assembly of the whole community (4:23; 14:27; 15:4)

3. Report of the latest events (4:23; 11:4; 12:17; 14:27; 15:4, 12, 14; 21:19)

4. Interpretation of those events as the works of God (14:27; 15:4, 12; 21:19)

5. Sequel: the community praises God (4:24-30; 11:18; 21:20)

According to Acts it seems that the early church not only celebrated the Eucharist; beyond that there were community assemblies in which events that were important to the community or that had happened in their missionary surroundings were interpreted as the works of God. It is clear that the subsequent praise of God therefore had a very different quality of enthusiasm. There was no longer anything schematic about it; it was tied to real community experiences and it touched matters affecting their own lives.

We may also say that the *Magnificat*, too, reflects community experiences, just as do the passages from Acts introduced above. It is worthwhile to take another look at it; after all, it does not just start somewhere or other. It begins with Mary's experience: "The Mighty One has done great things for me." But what sort of experience was it? Was it an isolated, utterly personal, individual experience that happened to Mary in the "silent chamber" of solitary interaction with God?

No, the story is quite different. An angel has to come and tell Mary what God plans for her and wants to do through her, and then Mary has to visit her cousin Elizabeth, who in turn has to greet her, saying "Blessed are you among women, and blessed is the fruit of your womb" (Luke 1:42). So here we have intensive communication, exchange, encounter—and only as a result of all that is Mary's song of praise made possible. But the communicative exchange is much broader, for Mary does not restrict her *Magnificat* to her own personal experience. Her praise extends over the whole history of Israel, expanding to include all that God had done in Israel since Abraham. That breadth is expressed in the *Magnificat* by its framing between two statements:

> He has looked with favor on the lowliness of his *servant*. (v. 48)

> He has helped his *servant* Israel. (v. 54)

The two words for "servant" are paired, as are "looked" and "helped," creating a genuine frame. What began with Abraham is completed in Mary and her child. God's action in Israel and God's action in Mary are firmly tied together.

The link reflected here in the *Magnificat* applies to every Christian: the great historical experiences of the People of God are only alive for them if they have experienced salvation in their own lives. On the other hand, they will be able to have, and especially to *interpret*, such personal experiences in the general context if they are rooted in the framework of the experience of the People of God, or at least live within the sphere of their influence.

It is the same with praise: the great celebration of God in the church's liturgy can be understood only by those who repeatedly experience in their own lives that God is acting in them, helping them, bringing them out of crisis. Then personal, spontaneous praise of God will be possible and be able to undergird and sustain liturgical praise. Every Christian should be able to say of herself or himself:

> The Mighty One has done great things for me,
> and holy is God's name.

The reverse is also true: individual praise will in most cases happen only if the individual is at home in the church's regular liturgical praise. To put it another way: while one must have experienced God's help "in the flesh" if praise is to move from the lips to the heart, one must live as a member of "the body of the church" in order to experience and communicate what happens to her or him personally.

Has this chapter turned praise into an infinitely complicated and thoroughly difficult thing? That would be a shame, because at heart it is really quite simple. We only need to praise God whenever there is cause to do so. Much of what we experience daily can turn into praise, and if that happens we will most certainly grow more and more into the church's liturgical worship as—beyond and apart from all immediate occasion—it praises the Father with Christ.

One thing is certain: someday our petitions and laments will fall silent, but the praise of God will never cease. Eternal life is pure praise.

*Chapter 5*

# Should We Ask for Things in Prayer?

According to a much-quoted aphorism of Walter Kasper, prayer is "the emergency tool of Christian faith." It is like a hot spot where all the problems of today's crisis of faith melt together. If prayer is the emergency tool of Christian faith, then petition is certainly central. It is, we might say, the critical part of the emergency tool.

## The crisis of petition

The size of this crisis of crises is evident here especially. More and more Christians, including believers, are asking themselves: is there any sense in praying for things? Is it right to ask God for something? If God were to hear my prayer, wouldn't that mean that God might intervene in the running of the world? Doesn't someone who asks God for something want God to change the course of history because of that prayer? But does God do such a thing? May God do that? We have seen that such questions have been virulent in Europe and North America since the Enlightenment, and they make our heads spin.

Some years ago a scholar suggested making a map of Germany that would show the frequency of storm damage from place to place: for example, fields swept by floods, regional flooding, buildings destroyed by lightning. Alongside that would be a map of the regions in which the blessing for good weather was given at the end of Sunday Mass and processions marched through the fields to pray for weather that enabled a fruitful harvest.

The scholar prophesied that bad weather would occur just as often in places where people regularly prayed for good weather as in those where such prayers had long been abandoned. More than that: he opined that in Roman Catholic Upper Bavaria, especially in the region around the Chiemsee, thunderstorms would be particularly frequent and strong, for meteorological reasons, no matter how often people prayed for favorable weather. Incidentally, the scholar who suggested these comparative maps was a theologian.

Not everyone would take his suggestion seriously, any more than they would give credence to the experiments by the American cardiologist Herbert Benson, who sought to demonstrate scientifically that bypass patients for whom prayers were offered would heal much faster than those for whom no prayers were said. His tests took place in six hospitals in the United States between 1998 and 2000. Benson separated 1,800 patients into three groups of equal size. The first group were assured that they were being prayed for. The second group were told that someone *might* be praying for them. No prayers were offered for the third group, and that message was conveyed to them. Interestingly, the degree of healing was worst in the group who were being prayed for—probably because the news that someone was praying for them caused those patients to become anxious. Critics rightly said that the whole experiment was senseless because it was burdened by too many unknowns.

There was, however, a test that was much more realistic, much more dreadful, and much more easily controlled. Hitler and his subordinates murdered six million Jews, many of whom were believers, and a great number of those constantly prayed to God to rescue them. Did God help them? They were selected, gassed, burned, their ashes scattered to the wind. Did God intervene in the course of history then?

When an earthquake brought a heavy church roof down on a nave full of people praying and killed them it was an outrage that was very hard to deal with. Auschwitz was much more so. Ever since the Lisbon earthquake on November 1, 1755, and most certainly since the *Shoah*, prayers of petition have become problematic, and with them belief in God—in a living God who acts in history.

## Petition as an expansion of consciousness?

There is one position—we already encountered it briefly above—that wants to clear out the whole problem from the roots up. It simply assigns a different role to petition. Its purpose is by no means to move God to do something, certainly not to change God. Its only purpose is to change the petitioner. When we pray to God for others, or for ourselves, we should notice that we have to change ourselves. Prayer of petition should confront us with the will of God and thereby make us aware that it is our own duty to act in the world.

Here is an example: there is not much point in praying for hungry people unless afterward we ourselves do something about hunger in the world. Those who do nothing for the hungry except to pray for them use prayer purely as an excuse, a substitute for action—or rather, for nonaction. Prayer for the hungry only makes sense if it awakens our social conscience. Our *prayer* for the hungry must lead to *action* for them. Only then is it legitimate.

There is a great deal to be said for that. I have no doubt of it. Those who pray honestly do change themselves in the process—or, better, they let themselves be changed by their petitions. And insofar as they let themselves be changed, God can act in the world through them. That is most certainly an aspect of prayer that is still underestimated. It was not God who ignored Auschwitz. We Christians did it.

But is that the whole story? Is there no purpose for petition other than to change ourselves? Is its function purely didactic? In that case doesn't it threaten to tip over into the mere expansion of consciousness? And if that is so, wouldn't it be better to get people together to share information than to engage in prayer?

I first became suspicious when I noticed that the petitions and Prayers of the People in the liturgy that were encumbered by the theory of petition I have been describing were growing more and more moralistic and instructive. This was the time of the "political night prayers" that began in October 1968 in the Church of St. Anthony in Cologne. What was begun there by Dorothee Sölle, Fulbert Steffensky, Marie Veit, Heinrich Böll, and Egbert Höflich was imitated in many places, consciously or unconsciously. It made its way into more and more prayer litanies and prayers composed by individuals.

Gradually it became clear to me that the purpose of these prayers was to reeducate me. They were constantly teaching. They wanted to offer me short lectures. Their real addressee was no longer God, but me, the one to be instructed. Formally, of course, they were addressed to God, who was, as usual, invoked at the beginning. But that was only cosmetic packaging. The prayer was not an appeal to God but instruction to be delivered to me, the one praying. And at that point those prayers began to get on my nerves.

My primary purpose in praying is not to receive instruction. I want to stand before God, call to God, pour out my heart before God. I want to complain to God, admit my own weakness. I want to admit that God is greater than I am. If all that succeeds in educating and changing me, fine and good. But the foreground in prayer should not be occupied by theological instruction.

As that became more and more clear to me I grew more and more grateful for the Psalms, and my respect for the genre of the Roman collects, with their depth and conciseness, greatly increased. Certainly there are also psalms that instruct, and obviously the Roman collects were and are partly intended to educate the assembled congregation: that is, to educate them toward a larger image of God and God's works of salvation. But they avoid the mistake of clothing themselves in pedagogy and urgent moral teaching. They address God as the Holy One who is greater than our hearts and whose actions in the world far surpass our own abilities.

## In the day of tribulation

Prayer of petition is a basic phenomenon in the Old Testament, present everywhere and always. Anyone in Israel who is in need cries out to God. That is so elementary and obvious that there is no need to think much about it. It is also a primal human reaction, one that breaks out everywhere and repeatedly in the world in spite of all rational objections.

During World War II, when people often sat by night in the often poorly protected "air-raid shelters" and heard the carpet bombing in progress overhead, the explosions coming closer and closer, many began to pray. Usually they prayed aloud, as in antiquity and the Ancient Near East, when prayers had almost always been vocal. That in itself showed that this was elementary prayer drawn from the depths of human crisis.

Petition in the Old Testament is elementary in the same sense. The one praying brings her or his whole existence before God. Petitioning God in prayer can be called "laying one's cries before God," "pouring out one's heart before God," "calling," "crying out," "groaning," and "weeping," often not referring to accompanying actions but to the prayer itself. Consider the so-called "salvation-historical creed" in Deuteronomy 26:5-10: "we cried to the LORD, the God of our ancestors; the LORD heard our voice and saw our affliction, our toil, and our oppression" (v. 7). Crying out to God when one is in need is simply a matter of course throughout the Old Testament. Many of the 150 psalms, or at least passages within them, are petitions.

But the Old Testament also offers reflections on petitionary prayer. Let me quote just one text, from Psalm 50. It is found in the context of a passage that reflects on proper sacrifices, and it says quite tersely: "Call on me in the day of trouble; I will deliver you, and you shall glorify me" (v. 15). This is addressed to all the people of Israel. "You" is the People of God. Israel is to bring God proper, acceptable offerings, namely, those that gather people into community—and essentially to a common feast at which thanks are offered to God for divine saving intervention.

In the next chapter we will have more to say about this kind of thanksgiving sacrifice. Here let me just say briefly how we ought to imagine such a thank-offering: an individual or a group of people have been in crisis. They begged God for help and solemnly promised that if they received God's help they would offer an animal sacrifice. God helped them, and now they have gathered in the forecourt of the temple, the sacrificial animal has been slaughtered, and people are sitting together, enjoying their meal. Then comes the decisive moment: the one who made the vow tells the story of the crisis and reports to those gathered how God helped in her or his hour of need.

Psalm 50 appears to favor that kind of sacrifice, the kind that brought people in Israel together to give thanks *in common*. It is precisely in that context that the psalm generalizes, in a kind of theological reflection, and has God say: "Call on me in the day of trouble; I will deliver you, and you shall glorify me." So God takes action when Israel calls for help. God has mercy. God saves, and praise arises as a response.

## Limitless trust

Jesus assumes all that as a matter of course. For him there is no question that human beings must constantly bring their petitions before God. Moreover, Jesus himself prayed, not only on the cross and not only in his hour of need on the Mount of Olives. The gospels clearly reflect the fact that his whole life was accompanied by prayer (cp. esp. Mark 1:35; Luke 9:18, 28).

Jesus' existential affinity to prayers of petition is revealed also in his instructions on prayer. It is not only that the Our Father, which he taught his disciples as a kind of "model for prayer," was a prayer of asking; in his other teaching on prayer he speaks almost entirely about correct, theologically appropriate asking.

What is the focus of Jesus' instruction on prayer? It can be easily pinpointed: Jesus demanded of his hearers that they pray with limitless trust, based on the fact that God will hear every petition made in such confidence. We see this in a saying of Jesus transmitted by Mark and Matthew: "whatever you ask for in prayer, believe that you have received it, and it will be yours" (Mark 11:24; cp. Matt 21:11). A great many earlier translations have followed a flood of manuscript witnesses in smoothing the text to read "believe that you are receiving it," but the earliest and best manuscripts have the verb "receive" in the aorist—an expressive aorist that can be used to depict a future event as having already happened. So the NRSV reads "that you have received it," and a still more accurate translation would be "Believe that you have as good as received it." You couldn't put it any more radically. There is a saying in Isaiah that is just as radical: in the end time it will be so that the wolf and the lamb will feed together and there will be nothing bad in Israel and no working and toiling in vain; God will hear all prayers even before they are spoken, or while they are still being uttered: "Before they call I will answer, while they are yet speaking I will hear" (Isa 64:24).

For Jesus the end time predicted by Isaiah is already breaking forth. God knows what disciples need before they have even put words to it. Therefore they should pray not only with profound trust but also with an absolute assurance that they are being heard.

The saying of Jesus cited above is such a fixed component of primitive Christian tradition that even the Fourth Evangelist takes it up in no fewer than three passages, transforming it into post-Easter prayer "in the name of Jesus": "I will do whatever you ask in my name, so that the Father may be glorified in the Son. If in my name you ask [me][1] for anything, I will do it" (John 14:13-14; cp. 15:7; 16:23).

It seems that the gospels of both Mark and John assume that the disciples may in principle ask God, or Jesus, for "anything." I will return to this problem in more depth below. May one ask God for "anything"? That is one of the basic problems of petitionary prayer; at the same time it opens the way to answering the question whether God really hears all our petitions.

At this point we note, first of all, that the Jesus-saying quoted in Mark 11:24 demands trust without limit. Matthew 6:7-8 points in exactly the same direction. Here again, Isaiah 65:24 forms the background:

> When you are praying, do not heap up empty phrases as the Gentiles do; for they think that they will be heard because of their many words. Do not be like them, for your Father knows what you need before you ask him.

One of the great temptations in praying for something is to heap up a lot of words addressed to God. We could reduce that temptation

---

1. "Me" is absent from some manuscripts; see the notes to the NRSV *ad loc*. Translation LMM.

to a formula: the greater the quantity of prayer, the more certain it is to be heard!

In the temples of antiquity private prayer was also, in principle, uttered aloud; hence one could immediately experience any *polylogia*, making-many-words. Jesus had enough opportunity to get acquainted with that kind of pagan practice of prayer in Galilee. He probably observed for himself how pagans prayed with an enormous number of words and constant repetition.

Why did they do that? In the first place it was meant to draw the attention of the god to whom they were praying. The god had to be persuaded to listen. That was the first thing. The second thing they wanted to achieve with their many words was that the god's or goddess's heart would be softened and the wish being expressed in the prayer would be fulfilled.

There was a common phrase in antiquity that gradually became a fixed formula. We find it in the works of Livy, Horace, Tacitus, Seneca. It reads *fatigare deos*, meaning: pray so as to tire out the god, to soften him or her up, so to speak, until he or she finally listens to the one praying.

When Jesus said that in praying one ought not make many words as the Gentiles do, certainly he was not simply opposing long prayers, or passionate prayers in which human beings pour out their whole hearts before God. What he rejects is simply the kind of prayer that regards the labor of praying as the real reason why the prayer is heard.

For Jesus the ultimate reason why "prayers are heard" is above all the goodness of the heavenly Father who already knows what the praying person needs. That by no means declares petitionary prayers superfluous; it gives them their proper basis. Every prayer is, after all, sustained by a limitless trust in the goodness of God, and such trust does not create empty words or require endless repetitions. But it must be spoken.

Trust in God is, in fact, the central subject of Jesus' instruction in prayer. This is evident also from Matthew 7:7-11, which stems from the Sayings Source (Q):

> Ask, and it will be given you; search, and you will find; knock, and the door will be opened for you. For everyone who asks

receives, and everyone who searches finds, and for everyone who knocks, the door will be opened. Is there anyone among you who, if your child asks for bread, will give a stone? Or if the child asks for a fish, will give a snake? If you then, who are evil, know how to give good gifts to your children, how much more will your Father in heaven give good things to those who ask him!

This prayer instruction begins with three imperatives: "ask," "search," "knock." The consequence—"it will be given you," "you will find," "the door will be opened for you"—follows directly after its respective imperative. The certainty with which hearing follows asking could not be expressed in more succinct and precise language. The double metaphor at the end of the instruction shows the reason for that assurance: the goodness of the heavenly Father, who cannot be surpassed in love and care by any earthly father.

From a rhetorical point of view the double metaphor works with a conclusion from the greater to the lesser: if even human beings—here Jesus' judgment is very realistic (they are evil)—if even they give good things to their children, then most certainly the heavenly Father does.

### Assurance of being heard

The similitude of the friend who is asked for help in the night in Luke 11:5-8 also uses high rhetorical style. Verses 5-7 constitute a continuous question that can be paraphrased as follows (with help from Joachim Jeremias):

> Can any of you imagine having a friend who would come to you at midnight and say: "Friend, lend me three loaves of bread, because a friend of mine has stopped with me on his journey and I haven't anything to offer him," and the one of you inside would answer, "Leave me alone; the door is already locked and my children are in bed with me; I can't get up and give you anything"—could you really imagine that?

The answer to that rhetorical question was obvious to Jesus' hearers. The refusal to help in such a situation was utterly unthinkable.

Near Eastern hospitality and the associated readiness to help simply did not permit it.

So the original point of Luke 11:5-7 was not to urge constant and urgent petition; it was to make it clear that human beings can have profound trust in God. Joachim Jeremias rightly formulated the thrust of the similitude thus:

> If the friend, roused from sleep in the middle of the night, does not hesitate for an instant to fulfill the petition of the neighbor in trouble, even though opening the bolt will wake the whole family—how much more God! [God] hears those in need. [God] helps them.

The parable of the unjust judge in Luke 18:1-8 points in precisely the same direction: a corrupt and unjust judge will not do right by a widow. But ultimately he does it—simply because the woman annoys him.

Of course, the original parable by no means intends to say that we should be as persistent and urgent in our petitions to God as the widow was to the judge, namely: if you are just as impertinent toward God, God will ultimately hear you. It is true that Luke pointed the parable in that direction by means of the narrative frame he put before and after it: "Then Jesus told them a parable about their need to pray always and not to lose heart" (Luke 18:1). But that interpretation did not touch the real meaning of the parable. By analogy to the similitude of the urgent friend Jesus would have told the parable to make this point:

> If a godless man like that judge finally does right by a widow for whom he cares not in the least, how much more will God come to the aid of those who call?

The major figure in the parable is not the widow, with her persistence, but the judge who is begged for help, just as in Luke 11:5-8 it is the friend who is asked for aid. So this parable also urges unlimited trust in God. Its original subject was not stubborn prayer but the sound confidence of being heard that disciples may enjoy because of the goodness of God.

In summary we may say that instructions on the right way to petition play an extraordinarily large role in the Jesus tradition. They occupy a good deal more space than we might expect. Among all those instructions the direction to pray with confidence is central. Its basis is the message of God's parental kindness.

Is there any point in further discussion of the question of the meaning of prayer of petition, given Jesus' clear position? Doesn't the clarity of his stance take care of the problems people have today with petitionary prayer? Can we even go on asking whether our petitions are really heard? Must we not say: because Jesus not only assumes petitionary prayer as a matter of course but constantly urges it, the last word has been said on the matter?

That is certainly true. Likewise, the fact that Jesus himself prayed lends a profound security to our own prayers. Even so, we cannot leave it at that. It is the task of theology to probe deeper and deeper, to never cease questioning.

Consequently the chapter on prayers of petition cannot end at this point. Let me begin all over again, and this time with the question: May we really pray for anything and everything, or only for particular things? That question leads further than we might think at first. It will, in fact, open to us a new horizon regarding the question whether and to what extent God really hears our prayers.

## What we may pray for

I have quoted Jesus' words in Mark 11:24: "*whatever* you ask for in prayer, believe that you have received it, and it will be yours." According to that we may pray for anything and everything; no restrictions are given. But that seems to contradict the Our Father, and we have to deal with that issue. We cannot avoid confronting it, because Jesus considered the Our Father the standard for right praying. It is the authoritative prayer for the group of disciples and for the People of God to be gathered anew; it is the pattern for prayer as such. But does the Our Father ask for anything and everything?

Apparently it does not. For example, it does not ask for long life. It does not ask for health or the healing of the sick, nor does it ask for rich harvests. It doesn't even ask for peace. What does the Our Father ask for? To summarize: it asks for the coming of the reign of God and nothing else.

But we have to give more precise reasons for saying that, since most interpretations of the Our Father have always said that the prayer has two parts. In the first part we pray for the coming of the reign of God, in three stages:

> Hallowed be thy name!
> Thy kingdom come!
> Thy will be done!

In these first three petitions the prayer looks only to God; it is, so to speak, about God's concerns. But then, in the second part, the Our Father shifts its perspective and now looks also to human concerns: for daily bread, for forgiveness of sins, and that they may not fall into temptation. And the petition for daily bread includes all the other cares that might afflict human beings. So the fourth petition of the Our Father, in particular, widens the horizon to the multiple needs of human beings, including the material ones.

In this way the Our Father teaches us the correct sequence for our prayers: first we must make God's concerns our own, but then all our particular needs come into play. First place always belongs to prayer for the *bona aeterna*, "the eternal goods," but then we may also pray for the *bona temporalia*, "temporal goods." We can read that advice over and over again in the many interpretations of the Our Father, or hear them in homilies.

Obviously there is a good deal of truth in it: for example, that the Our Father clearly has two parts, the first one dominated by the second-person-singular "you" ("thy": so "hallowed be thy name," "thy kingdom come," "thy will be done"), the second by the first-person-plural "we" (our bread, our sins, lead us not).

It is also correct that the first three petitions are all about one thing: the coming of the reign of God. The three petitions develop three aspects, but in fact they are all about the reign of God.

Finally, it is likewise correct that as regards the first part of the Our Father we can speak of "God's concerns." The one praying is to enter into what concerns God and what God wills.

The whole thing becomes false only at the point where the second part of the Our Father is sharply distinguished from the first part: now the subject is no longer God's concerns but "human cares," and the fourth petition is, so to speak, only about the sum of human concerns.

It is precisely at this point that the traditional interpretation usually overlooks that, in the first place, the Our Father is a prayer designed for Jesus' disciples—a prayer that reflects those disciples' specific situation. The fourth petition is not on behalf of starving nations, of "bread for the world," of rich harvests from the fields; it is about disciples who are traveling through Israel and often do not know in the morning where they will be housed at night or whether they will have enough bread for the next day.

Why are Jesus' disciples traveling? Why aren't they carrying backpacks full of provisions? Why don't they make plans and concern themselves with their daily needs? It is because they are traveling to proclaim the reign of God everywhere in Israel and that proclamation must be their only concern.

Moreover, Jesus' disciples do not pray for their "daily bread"— that is a wrong translation—but for bread for "the day to come," that is, for a single day. They are not to pray for more than that.

The bread petition in the Our Father does not suddenly introduce a new topic, that of human concerns of the sort that burden everyone. The Our Father hews steadfastly to its single theme: the coming of the reign of God. In the second part of the prayer Jesus' disciples ask that everything that makes possible the coming of the reign of God may take place in their midst.

*First*, they ask God that they may constantly find friends and sympathizers who will give them shelter and bread at night so that in the morning they can move on, unburdened, and proclaim the reign of God.

*Second*, they ask God to free them, again and again, from their guilt and unforgiveness, for how can they plausibly proclaim the reign of God if strife and rivalry are at work among them?

*Third*, they ask God not to lead them into temptation, that is, into a situation in which they will be tested beyond their strength—one that is too hard to withstand. Ultimately this sixth petition in the

Our Father seems to be about not letting them be unfaithful to their calling for the sake of the reign of God.

## Only "spiritual goods"?

We asked ourselves: may we pray for everything? To find an answer we turned our eyes to the Our Father, because it is a model for prayer that teaches us how we ought to pray. And there it appeared that the Our Father is exclusively about the coming of the reign of God, even in the petitions in the second part, for those petitions are meant to make it possible for Jesus' disciples to live in right relationship to the reign of God and precisely in that way to bear witness to God's rule.

If we follow the pattern of the Our Father it seems as if we may not pray for everything but only for the coming of God's reign and for what coincides with life under the rule of God. Other New Testament texts point in the same direction; for example, Matthew 6:33 contains a Jesus-saying: "strive first for the kingdom of God and his righteousness, and all these things will be given you as well." It is clear from the context in which the *logion* is placed what "all these things" are. Jesus' disciples should not ask: "What are we to eat? What are we to drink? What are we to put on?" The Gentiles are concerned about "all these things." God knows that they need them. Instead, they should concern themselves with the reign of God and nothing else.

All these things—those are the so-called "temporal goods"— will be given them besides. But no one needs to pray for what will be given in any case. Doesn't that say with utter clarity that we should pray not for "temporal goods" but only for the coming of the reign of God?

When we think of the trajectory of Matthew 6:33 and the Our Father, another text springs to mind. We have already seen it: it was the twofold metaphor of the stone and the serpent. There we read:

> Is there anyone among you who, if your child asks for bread, will give a stone? Or if the child asks for a fish, will give a snake? If you then, who are evil, know how to give good gifts to your

children, how much more will your Father in heaven give good things to those who ask him! (Matt 7:9-11)

Luke knew that text from the so-called Sayings Source (Q) but changed it in a number of places. One of those changes is theologically significant. Matthew's text says that God will give "good things" to those who ask. Luke writes instead:

If you then, who are evil, know how to give good gifts to your children, how much more will the heavenly Father give the *Holy Spirit* to those who ask him! (Luke 11:13)

It would seem that Luke's changing the text touched precisely the problem we are considering: may we really ask God for everything? Does God fulfill every request?

Luke knew Israel's Scriptures. He was aware that Solomon, when God offered to grant his request, did not pray for long life, or for honor and wealth, but for an "understanding mind"[2] and for wisdom and discernment. God was pleased, and God fulfilled Solomon's wish, giving him also what he certainly had not consciously asked for (1 Kgs 3:5-15).

Against that background Luke evidently found the formulation "receive good things from God" too vague. What we ought to ask for, according to Luke, is the Holy Spirit, and we will receive it. God will never refuse us the Holy Spirit.

It seems that Luke's idea lies precisely on the track that is visible in the Our Father as well. We may pray for God's Holy Spirit, we may pray for spiritual goods, we may pray for the coming of God's reign, we may pray for everything that testifies to the coming of that reign—but we should not pray for "temporal goods" such as long life, health, honor, wealth, and many other like items.

## The dilemma

That, however, confronts us with a real dilemma: it is not only that every saying of Jesus we have consulted sets no boundaries and

---

2. NRSV. Other translations read "a listening heart." Translation LMM.

says that we may ask for everything—for example: "So I tell you, whatever you ask for in prayer, believe that you have received it, and it will be yours" (Mark 11:24).

Indeed, it is a fact that our whole faith-filled existence resists any limitation on our prayers of petition to purely spiritual goods. Obviously it is clear to us that we may not ask anything nonsensical or immoral from God. We cannot ask that God will let us pass an exam even though, out of pure laziness, we haven't moved a finger to prepare for it. We most certainly may not ask God to make a competitor of ours unable to work so that we can advance our own career. Such prayer would be nothing more nor less than blasphemy.

In principle every one of us senses that we may not pray for nonsense or for what is immoral. But beyond the things that simply do not belong before God there are broader realms in which we ask God for help—often quite spontaneously but frequently out of profound need. "God, help me to survive," prays a mountain climber overtaken by a fast-moving cold front and suddenly hanging on an ice-clad wall of rock. "Oh, God, let that child be all right," prays a driver who has struck a child—a driver who really was driving carefully, and yet the child suddenly darted into the street from between two parked cars.

Are such prayers wrong, because they do not ask for spiritual goods? Are they theologically inappropriate? Is it right to denounce such prayers and so to limit and narrow the sphere of petitions? Does that do justice to real persons, given that, on the other hand, teachers of the spiritual life also say that one should be in constant conversation with God? Doesn't that also mean constant thanks and constant petitioning?

Thérèse of Lisieux (1873–1897), who entered Carmel at the age of fifteen, tells how she wished for snow on the day she would receive the habit:

> I wanted to see Nature clad like myself, in white, on my Clothing Day, but I had almost given up hope because it was so warm the day before that it might have been spring.
>
> The 10th came, and the weather was just the same, so I gave up my childish desire as impossible of realization.

But then, when she had been dressed in her white robe and returned from the church to the cloister,

> I turned towards the quadrangle and—*I saw that it was completely covered in snow!* What delicacy on the part of Jesus! To gratify His little bride's every desire, He had sent her snow![3]

Probably Thérèse was much too tactful to pray explicitly for snow, but she wished for it, and when the mild weather suddenly turned and snow really fell she received it as "delicacy on the part of Jesus" for her festal day.

I say all that only to make it clear that before God there are longings, hopes, wishes, even petitions that go far beyond prayers in crisis or in need. Is that broad meadow of encounter between God and the individual supposed to be fenced off? Shouldn't one be allowed to pray in such fields? Was the silent wish for snow in the heart of this young woman who wanted to serve God in Carmel with her whole existence somehow deviant, senseless, not theologically appropriate?

Somehow I am resistant to any attempt to draw a clear line limiting the scope of petition. Wouldn't that in some way smother my relationship to God? But that only makes our problem that much bigger. What is the solution? On the one hand, we have the instinctive knowledge that we may storm God with everything, and on the other hand, we have the model of the Our Father, directed entirely to the reign of God. How can we escape that dilemma?

## The all-encompassing nature of the reign of God

The solution lies in the Our Father itself. It remains true that the Our Father prays for the coming of the reign of God and nothing else. But—what is the reign of God, after all?

---

3. Thérèse of Lisieux, *The Story of a Soul: The Autobiography of the Little Flower*, ed. Mother Agnes of Jesus, trans. Michael Day (Charlotte, NC: Saint Benedict Press, 2010), 91–92.

The reign of God does *not* refer to a higher world; it means this world in which we live. It does not describe a world beyond, but rather the here and now; it is not heaven but earth. When the Johannine Jesus says to Pilate, "My kingdom is not from this world" (John 18:36), he by no means intends to say that it is somewhere outside this world but instead that it is different from this world's societies and groups. It does not correspond to the usual social structures because in it no violence is exercised.

The reign of God that Jesus proclaims, however, likewise does not mean something purely invisible, a merely internal realm, something within the soul, hidden and inaccessible. Martin Luther interpreted the Greek *entos hymōn* in Luke 17:21 that way, translating "*Das Reich Gottes ist inwendig in euch* [The kingdom of God is within you]," but that was certainly incorrect.[4] In the context Jesus is being asked by Pharisees about when the reign of God will come. He answers them by saying that it will not come in such a way that it can be determined by particular signs. No one will be able to say, "Look here!" or "Look there!" and that is because it is (already) "among you." It may be that *entos hymōn* intends to say that the reign of God is "accessible" to you, it is (already) "available." At any rate, *entos* in ancient business documents surviving on papyrus points in that direction. However that may be, Jesus in no way saw the already-inbreaking reign of God as a purely internal event. No indeed:

> the blind receive their sight, the lame walk, the lepers are cleansed, the deaf hear, the dead are raised, the poor have good news brought to them. (Luke 7:22)

These things are happening for all to see. The reign of God is breaking into the midst of this world, and not just into its interior life. The world is to be transformed, and no sphere of it can be left out. All dimensions of reality are to be placed under God's rule: soul and body, health and sickness, wealth and poverty, family and society.

---

4. The revised German version of Luther's Bible (1984) and the *Einheitsübersetzung* now read "*Das Reich Gottes ist mitten unter euch*" ("The kingdom of God is in your midst [or: among you]"). This parallels exactly the movement from the Authorized ("King James") Version to the NRSV. Translation LMM.

From that perspective every prayer for the coming of the reign of God acquires a comprehensive extent, and in turn everything a person asks for in crisis becomes part of the inbreaking reign of God. The distinction between "temporal" and "eternal" goods suddenly ceases to function—and that is because both the "temporal" and the "worldly" are also to be transformed by the power of God's reign.

Because that is the case we may also pray for temporal and worldly things to the extent that such a prayer serves the reign of God, so long as it is open to the transformation of the world that coincides with the coming of the reign of God. All that sounds very theoretical, and so I will use an example to show what I mean.

## A fatal disease

Someone is sick, very sick. Every effort to master the illness has so far failed. Doctors cannot help. The sick person prays for health; friends and acquaintances join in that prayer. The more the disease develops, the more urgent the prayers of the sufferer and the friends become. God must help; God must save the sick person.

Question: Is such prayer allowed? Is it biblical? Is it appropriate? Does it accord with Jesus' teaching on prayer? The answer can only be: obviously!—for the reign of God is not just about spiritual goods. It is also about the body and its needs. After all, Jesus repeatedly healed sick persons for that very reason, and for the same reason he was shaken by the death of his friend Lazarus.

Besides, it might be that the sick person of whom I have spoken, if healed, will be able to increase the use of her or his strength on behalf of the church and thus for the reign of God. Or it may be that the healing will be a sign of God's caring nearness, both for the sick person and for others who learn of it. We can imagine many ways in which this prayer for healing may be profoundly connected with the coming of the reign of God. Jesus, at any rate, counted his healings of sick persons among the signs of the imminent arrival of the reign of God.

But let us suppose for the moment that all the sick person's prayers for healing produce no result. The illness develops further. The doctors' efforts are now directed only at combating the increasing pain. The sufferer becomes visibly weaker and has long since begun to think of dying, although there are repeated moments in which new hope seems to arise. Should this person go on praying to be healed?

In fact, that is what happens. The sufferer continues to pray for a semi-miraculous event, for a physician who knows more than the others, a medicine that might still work. But the prayers begin to change, without her noticing it. They are now more and more often also about patience, about being able to hold out, about surrender, and about consolation for those who love her.

At some point this prayer enters a final phase. Now she prays less and less for herself and more and more for others as she considers whether her illness and steadily approaching death might have some meaning. She tries to discover the sense of it. Might the sufferings she is enduring somehow help to heal a deep discord or rupture within her family? Now her prayer changes yet again, and in the end her dying becomes a single prayer, almost without words.

Does all that have anything to do with the reign of God? Well, obviously! And it also has a great deal to do with the salvation that comes with the reign of God since, while the sick person has not been healed, she has become whole.

I have used this example to make it clear that everything we encounter, everything that comes to meet us, may be connected to the reign of God. The separation between *bona temporalia* and *bona aeterna*, between "temporal" and "eternal" goods, is unsustainable. Even the pairing of the two is false. The reign of God presses into time. It intends to transform the world. So "eternal" and "temporal" constantly run into each other. The reign of God contains everything, and therefore we may pray for everything. All prayers can further God's cause.

## Problem: are our prayers heard?

What we have just said thrusts us into the center of the question of whether our prayers are heard. Did God hear the prayer of the sick person described above? She first prayed for health, but

God gave her wholeness in a more profound sense. God heard the prayers, though not in the way the sick person first hoped. We need to consider these connections more closely.

We began with a dilemma: that, on the one hand, we may pray for everything and, on the other hand, that God can only receive our prayers when they are in accordance with the reign of God—when they are connected with God's desire to heal and save the world, thus transforming it. We might say that the real problem, the real difficulty about our petitions, is that we often do not know whether our urgent begging really has anything to do with the reign of God and so with God's will.

That concern is scarcely visible, if at all, in the church's prayers of petition. When we pray for good bishops, more priests and pastors, the faith of our young people, just government, or help for the hungry, such prayers are always right and are quite obviously related to the coming of the reign of God.

It is much more problematic, though, when prayer touches my own behavior, my own decisions, my own existence. Here I cannot know in advance what is appropriate to the reign of God and so corresponds to God's will. What about Jesus' prayers on the Mount of Olives, for example? What did he pray for? Mark's gospel says:

> They went to a place called Gethsemane; and he said to his disciples, "Sit here while I pray." He took with him Peter and James and John, and began to be distressed and agitated. And he said to them, "I am deeply grieved, even to death; remain here, and keep awake." And going a little farther, he threw himself on the ground and prayed that, if it were possible, the hour might pass from him. He said, "Abba, Father, for you all things are possible; remove this cup from me; yet, not what I want, but what you want." (Mark 14:32-36)

The text is utterly clear: Jesus was overcome by fear of death. This is not just the so-called "creaturely" fear that shakes a person so thoroughly that he is no longer in control of his limbs. The fear seized Jesus' spirit as much as his body.

Jesus prays that "this cup" might be removed from him. "This cup" is arrest, trial, execution. Jesus did not create any illusions for himself; he saw all that approaching. But at the same time "this cup" is his death as an evil laid upon him by God. Let's be blunt: Jesus doesn't want to die.

So on the Mount of Olives—to use the classic terminology for the moment—Jesus prays for a "temporal," a "worldly," good. He begs to be rescued from the threat of death. Did his heavenly Father hear him? Apparently not: Jesus was seized, tried, ridiculed, lashed till his blood ran, and executed.

But still, the letter to the Hebrews says that the hour on the Mount of Olives must be seen against the background of Jesus' whole existence. (It speaks of "the days of his flesh.") God most certainly did hear Jesus' prayers and pleading. The text that is the climax of the theology of Hebrews reads:

> In the days of his flesh, Jesus offered up prayers and supplications, with loud cries and tears, to the one who was able to save him from death, and he was heard because of his reverent submission. Although he was a Son, he learned obedience through what he suffered; and having been made perfect, he became the source of eternal salvation for all who obey him. (Heb 5:7-9)

This text, with its incomparably radical theology, says as clearly as can be how God heard the passionate prayer of the Son: Jesus was made perfect. That is: Jesus was snatched out of death, elevated to the status of High Priest, and so became the wholeness, the salvation, of the world.

But, Hebrews means to say, that would have been impossible if Jesus had not learned obedience through suffering. It was about the surrender of his life, and that surrender, that handing over of his own person, was not a matter of course. Everyone shrinks from it. Everyone would rather escape it. Jesus too had to learn to surrender himself.

Jesus' prayer was heard, Hebrews says, but it was heard differently from what the screaming and weeping Jesus would have wished. To put it in the words of Jesus' own preaching: God wanted to bring the kingdom into being, but it could not happen on a wave of success; it could only come in the form of lowliness. That gives the meaning of the reign of God a new definition. From then on the reign of God can no longer be thought of apart from its character as inconspicuous, unprepossessing, and even being mistaken for something else. The reign of God comes incognito.

That is the most profound reason why we so often do not know what corresponds to the reign of God, what is appropriate to it. It comes differently from the way we continually desire. Again and again it tosses aside our own ideas. It constantly reverses all our thinking.

Therefore all our asking and pleading must take place under the auspices of "Lord, may your will be done. Not what I will, but what you will." The whole Gethsemane scene in the Synoptic Gospels moves toward this surrender to the will of God. This is not the will of a tyrant who orders suffering for suffering's sake; it is the will of the omnipotent and merciful God who knows infinitely more about the world and history than we can. On this point Hebrews says substantially what the Synoptics say, but in this way: "Although he was a Son, he learned obedience through what he suffered."

So it remains true that we may pray for everything. It remains true that in crisis we may pray for our personal rescue. At any rate, Jesus did. It even remains true that God hears all our petitions. But God can only hear our petitions in such a way that God's listening is in accord with the coming of the reign of God, thus God's will to save the world.

There remains, then, a discrepancy between the way we imagine what it means to be heard and the way God actually fulfills our petitions. In that we continually add "not as I will, but as you will" we acknowledge that discrepancy. In doing so we meld our own much-shrunken view of what the reign of God is with God's point of view, and at the same time we humbly admit that God is greater than we are and sees more than we can see. Infinitely more.

## Jesus himself prayed

To conclude: prayer of petition is indispensable because it is the most elementary expression of the truth that God is personal: that is, that God wants to encounter us as a living "thou." But petitionary prayer is also an elementary acknowledgment that we ourselves come before God with our whole existence and recognize God as our creator and Lord. Petition is a gesture, a signpost without which the face of God would ultimately fade. And that is why prayers designed only to broaden my consciousness always irritate me whenever I hear them.

It is also very true that we cannot know *more* about God and human beings than Jesus did. If Jesus prayed—and that he did so is clear from the scene in the Garden of Olives—then it must be right to do so.

The great theologian Tertullian (ca. 160–220) ends his tractate *On Prayer*, which primarily deals with the Our Father, by saying simply:

> *Quid ergo amplius de officio orationis? Etiam ipse dominus oravit.*
> What more then, touching the office of prayer? Even the Lord
> Himself prayed. (*De oratione* 29)

For Tertullian that says it all, and in the end I cannot say more. Christian existence means unconditional adherence to Jesus. In him we have everything—and we have it infallibly.

*Chapter 6*

# Lament Is a Legitimate Form of Prayer

## Mourning rituals

Breaking into tears in public is something that makes a certain type of European shudder. They simply find it embarrassing. When they see on television how women in the East mourn a dead person, swaying back and forth, striking their breasts, ululating and crying aloud, they feel alienated. For centuries people like us have been brought up to be self-contained. Despite many counter-movements in European history, the ideals of the *Stoa* have held their place. True, in the sentimental eighteenth century there was a boom in weeping, even in Germany, but on the whole the Stoic ideals remained more powerful. How can anyone put his innermost feelings on public display?! Many of us think that way when we see Eastern mourning rituals, and in doing so we show that we have only understood half of what takes place in such rituals.

Obviously they display something. Sorrow must be shown; that is owed to the public. But saying that by no means explains everything. A lot more is going on. What is innermost is turned outward. Pain is allowed expression. An Eastern woman immerses herself in sorrow, and everyone among us who has seen how people can become sick with sorrow can understand that giving a shape and form to pain has a healing function. Those who sicken from sorrow have swallowed their pain, and now it is eating its way through their bodies.

In ancient Israel public mourning was a matter of course; no one was ashamed of it, and for the same reason no one was ashamed of raising laments before God. In the books of the Old Testament we find cries and songs of lament nearly everywhere. There is even an entire book—Lamentations—placed after Jeremiah, that consists of five "songs of lament" on the fall of the Southern Kingdom and the destruction of the temple (586 BCE).

Chapters 1, 2, and 4 of that biblical book use elements of ancient Near Eastern "city laments" in which the former glory of a destroyed city was sung and its current misery mourned. The city is always depicted as a woman, and the same is true in these three great songs of lament. Mourning for the dead is raised over the crushed city of Jerusalem. The first begins this way:

> How lonely sits the city
>    that once was full of people!
> How like a widow she has become,
>    she that was great among the nations!
> She that was a princess among the provinces
>    has become a vassal.
> She weeps bitterly in the night,
>    with tears on her cheeks.
>
> . . .
>
> The roads to Zion mourn,
>    for no one comes to the festivals;
> all her gates are desolate,
>    her priests groan;
> her young girls grieve,
>    and her lot is bitter.
> Her foes have become the masters,
>    her enemies prosper,
> because the LORD has made her suffer
>    for the multitude of her transgressions. (Lam 1:1-2, 4-5)

We can see immediately that this is a highly poetic text. The same is true of all the lament songs in the Old Testament. They are altogether poetic and yet they draw on everyday laments. They are styled with the utmost artistry, and yet they stem from genuine experience. A long period of European scholarship preached the foolish prejudice that stylized rituals were incompatible with genuine feeling.

## An African bride

Years ago I attended a double wedding of a German couple and an African couple, the latter from Tanzania. From the altar I was able to observe their faces, their posture, their body language.

The German couple stood close together. If they could have, they would have moved even closer. They had open faces; now and then they smiled at each other. When they sat down for the homily the bridegroom took care in arranging the bride's dress. They had to wait for their public kiss, but it was in the air.

With the Tanzanian couple it was entirely different, at least during their wedding. Both were very serious; their faces were closed. There was even a hint of sorrow on the bride's face. She never looked aside, never smiled at her groom; instead, she seemed to move away from him.

What an odd couple, I thought at the time: no joyfulness, not a sign of mutual trust. How untypical of Africans, I conjectured. Why is this bride so uptight? Only gradually did I come to realize what it all meant. It had nothing at all to do with being uptight. In the Near East (and the situation is similar in Africa) the bride leaves her parents' house and clan and transfers to her husband's family. From a sociological point of view that is a significant step. Psalm 45, a song of the messianic king and his bride, shows how weighty it always was. There the royal bride is consoled:

> Hear, O daughter, consider and incline your ear;
>    forget your people and your father's house,
>    and the king will desire your beauty.
> Since he is your lord, bow to him . . .

And the bridegroom is assured:

> In the place of ancestors you . . . shall have sons;
>    you will make them princes in all the earth. (Ps 45:10-11, 16)

So the king's bride—and that African woman as well—had to leave her father and her father's father and transfer to a family strange to her, and she is sad about it and must show her sorrow. She owes that to her old family. Woe to her if she should smile at that hour!

As I have said, that all occurred to me only as I thought about it afterward. Moreover, the behavior of that African bride also made it clear to me how ridiculous it is to play off ritual and genuine feeling against one another. Her attitude was highly stylized, but who will dare to say that it was "only" stylized, "only" a kind of theater, "only" demanded by her origins and upbringing and therefore was nothing but obligatory body language?

## Cast into the underworld

We can apply all that to the laments in the Psalter. They are entirely and exclusively stylized; they use fixed expressions from the construction set for mourning rituals; they hold to an already-existing generic style. They are often even prepared formulas that can be used in appropriate situations—and yet for those who "perform" them they are texts that strike to the marrow of one's bones. Even today they retain their power. Let us consider Psalm 88, a pure lament from beginning to end:

> [1]O LORD, God of my salvation,
>     when, at night, I cry out in your presence,
> [2]let my prayer come before you;
>     incline your ear to my cry.
> [3]For my soul is full of troubles,
>     and my life draws near to Sheol.
> [4]I am counted among those who go down to the Pit;
>     I am like those who have no help,
> [5]like those forsaken among the dead,
>     like the slain that lie in the grave,
> like those whom you remember no more,
>     for they are cut off from your hand.
> [6]You have put me in the depths of the Pit,
>     in the regions dark and deep.

⁷Your wrath lies heavy upon me,
  and you overwhelm me with all your waves.        *Selah*
⁸You have caused my companions to shun me;
  you have made me a thing of horror to them.
I am shut in so that I cannot escape;
  ⁹my eye grows dim through sorrow.
Every day I call on you, O LORD;
  I spread out my hands to you.
¹⁰Do you work wonders for the dead?
  Do the shades rise up to praise you?              *Selah*
¹¹Is your steadfast love declared in the grave,
  or your faithfulness in Abaddon?
¹²Are your wonders known in the darkness,
  or your saving help in the land of forgetfulness?
¹³But I, O LORD, cry out to you;
  in the morning my prayer comes before you.
¹⁴O LORD, why do you cast me off?
  Why do you hide your face from me?
¹⁵Wretched and close to death from my youth up,
  I suffer your terrors; I am desperate.
¹⁶Your wrath has swept over me;
  your dread assaults destroy me.
¹⁷They surround me like a flood all day long;
  from all sides they close in on me.
¹⁸You have caused friend and neighbor to shun me;
  [my one companion is darkness!][1]

There are few psalms that end so darkly. The last line declares that impenetrable darkness reigns. The one praying the psalm does express trust in God at the beginning, crying out to the "God of my salvation," and the style of the genre would lead us to expect that the psalm would somewhere speak of that salvation, yet precisely that is what never appears. The reader's expectations are disappointed. Here there is nothing about rescue, about salvation; there is only the crisis of death.

1. Last line from the author's German; trans. LMM. Cp. Robert Alter, *The Book of Psalms: A Translation with Commentary* (New York: W. W. Norton, 2007), 310: "My friends—utter darkness."

Psalm 89, which follows, does begin with a marvelous expression of praise, and someone praying the psalms and attending to the context might think that here, within the multivocal orchestration of the Psalter, a redeemed counterpart sings against Psalm 88:

> I will sing of your steadfast love, O Lord, forever;
>> with my mouth I will proclaim your faithfulness to all
>> generations.
> I declare that your steadfast love is established forever;
>> your faithfulness is as firm as the heavens. (Ps 89:1-2)

In reality the first part of Psalm 89 (vv. 1-37) only invokes God's past promises to David. Of the second part of the psalm (vv. 38-51) we can say that it contains not a trace of assurance. God has "spurned and rejected," has withdrawn the covenant and destroyed Jerusalem. Nothing remains but misery and suffering.

So in a broader view Psalm 89 extends the lament of Psalm 88. Both psalms are cries for help. Both invoke God's faithfulness. They want to believe in God's promises, but reality does not allow it. Still, because it closes the Third Book of Psalms (i.e., Pss 73–89), Psalm 89 has been given a solemn doxology at the end:

> Blessed be the Lord forever.
> Amen and Amen.

To that extent everything that precedes is nevertheless embedded in Israel's indestructible hope, but taken in itself Psalm 88 reveals almost nothing of it. Even the petitions, which otherwise may never be omitted in a song of lament, are reduced to the utter minimum. There is one plea near the beginning, in verse 2; otherwise this psalm is pure lament.

Even more than that, it is a relentless protest against a life like the one that has fallen upon the one praying (or upon Israel). This is the protest of a person with whom God refuses all communication and who has stood with one foot in the grave since youth. The whole psalm is infused with images of death; it speaks of the realm of the dead, the pit, the grave, dungeon, darkness, and the land of forgetfulness—and also of waves that drown the one praying. These are the primeval waters, an image of unavoidable destruction.

## A shadow existence

The supplicant cries to God day and night, but especially in the early morning because morning marks the end of night, the time when Old Testament worshipers expect God's saving intervention. But God does not intervene, and so there remains for the one crying for help only bitter irony:

> <sup>10</sup>Do you work wonders for the dead?
>   Do the shades rise up to praise you?            *Selah*
> <sup>11</sup>Is your steadfast love declared in the grave,
>   or your faithfulness in Abaddon?

Behind such challenging irony lies the conviction that in the realm of the dead a person only lives a pitiable shadow existence. There is no more life, not even speech—the dead only whisper (Isa 29:4)—and therefore there is no praise of God. If God now allows the supplicant to die, God will not only destroy a life that has never been allowed to be a real life but will silence a human being who wants to praise God.

If God lets the supplicant die? No, the psalm, and with it the whole of the Old Testament, thinks much more radically than that: one who is abandoned, persecuted, in misery, is vegetating, even *before* physical death, in the *sphere* of death. She already houses among shadows and has entered the "land of forgetfulness." Death has long since engulfed her.

This is especially evident in that the petitioner falls into profound loneliness. Friends abandon him; intimates withdraw from him. Even the members of his household are estranged. He is avoided; he is a marked man. Although the psalm does not say so, in the world at that time such social stigmatizing rested on the opinion that guilt lay upon anyone who had such bad fortune, either his own guilt or that of his ancestors. That led to distancing, conscious or unconscious. You have to be careful with such people; better to keep away from them. Reactions of that kind were common at the time. The book of Job pictures them vividly. Even Job's wife turns away from her husband. "Curse God, and die!" she tells him (Job 2:9).

## God the accused

What is most shocking about Psalm 88 and many other songs of lament in the Old Testament, however, is not the supplicant's social isolation; it is her isolation from and because of God. The whole complaint in Psalm 88 is saturated with the idea that God did all that: the divine face is hidden from me: that is, God has rejected me (v. 15); it is God who has brought me into isolation (v. 9); it is God who has laid the divine wrath upon me (v. 17); it is God who has cast me into the pit (v. 7). Lament before God becomes accusation against God, who appears not only as incomprehensible but as the enemy of the one praying.

May one pray that way? Is it permissible to complain in such a way? Are we allowed to accuse God? The Bible does it, at any rate. It does build in some barriers, setting such accusations in the context of trust and praise. Still, within that context there remains the unadorned accusation that defangs nothing, conceals nothing, and does not piously whitewash a single detail.

Again: is it permissible to pray that way? An initial answer could be that it is better to express one's protest than to carry it around inside oneself. It is better to accuse God than to slowly poison oneself with unspoken thoughts. Every psychologist would immediately agree, and there is a whole spectrum of psychological techniques that point in the same direction: to express one's rage, even to shout oneself hoarse to the depths of one's soul, in the presence of a professional. To a certain extent theologians have long since adopted the insights of current psychology; they say—quite rightly:

> that the God Yhwh is not the idol of an empty otherworldliness but a living Thou, a God to whom one can speak, who hears and allows himself to be challenged, a God to whom one may empty one's heart, to whom one may say anything and everything (without fear of misunderstanding and sanctions), one who even repents.[2]

---

2. Erich Zenger, *Psalmen. Auslegungen 1–4*, 2nd ed. (Freiburg: Herder, 2006), 179. Translation LMM. See also Frank-Lothar Hossfeld and Erich Zenger, *Psalms 2 (Psalms 51–100)*, trans. Linda M. Maloney, Hermeneia (Minneapolis: Fortress Press, 2005), 389–98.

All that is absolutely true, and a great deal more could be added in the same vein. Newer Psalms exegesis has, however, adopted an approach precisely with regard to the question we are considering that carries us a good deal farther. That approach posits persuasively that the Psalter is not a collection of isolated individual Psalms but a major, considered, and carefully coordinated composition. For example, the whole Psalter is intended to be a meditative response to the Sinai Torah. Therefore, like the Torah, it is made up of five books. Thus it places Psalm 1 at the beginning, as the entrance gate ("Happy are those . . . [whose] delight is in the law of the LORD, [on whose] law they meditate day and night"), and therefore Torah psalms are scattered throughout the Psalter.

But not only that!—an equally dominant and still more important theme finds its place, as a pointer, in Psalm 2: the messianic king. Messianic psalms appear repeatedly as strategic markers throughout the Psalter. Most important among these are Psalms 72, 89, 101, 110, and 144. This gives the entire Psalter a messianic substructure. That is no accident; it was meant to be.

The result, then, is that not only the individual and not only Israel prays these psalms: the hoped-for messianic king prays them together with his people, the king who will be installed by God and who will, once for all, lay all things at God's feet. That Messiah then speaks, together with Israel, not only praise and thanksgiving; he descends with his people into the suffering that is inflicted on them—including the suffering they bring on themselves through their internal enmities and rivalries. The Messiah will personally become the bearer of that suffering, and the Messiah laments with Israel before God. In this way all the laments in the Psalter acquire a depth that links the complaints of today's supplicants with the laments of Israel and Israel's Messiah. There is no song of lament in the Psalter that illustrates these connections more clearly than Psalm 22.

## A liturgy in Israel

To really understand Psalm 22 we need to make a short detour, because it presents itself in a form that at first is alienating, though it is one we often encounter in psalms of lament. What is unusual about Psalm 22 is the multiplicity of kinds of prayer it contains: lament ("My God, my God, why have you forsaken me?"), petition ("Do not be far from me, for trouble is near"), expression of trust ("Yet you are holy"), praise ("From you comes my praise in the great congregation"), and thanksgiving ("he did not despise or abhor the affliction of the afflicted").

In any case that spectrum is striking, but still more so is the following observation: the supplicant's attitude shifts surprisingly in verse 22 from the most profound lament to praise and thanksgiving. That is unexpected. How does such a reversal happen? It probably can be explained only if there was a situation in the life of ancient Israel in which lament suddenly turned to thanksgiving. Had there been such a situation? Evidently! Contemporary interpreters of the Bible are nearly unanimous on this point. The situation was the so-called *tôdā*-liturgy, though we have to reconstruct it. *Tôdā* is a Hebrew word meaning to give thanks, to bring a thank-offering. What was the occasion for such a liturgy of thanksgiving, and how did it look? Probably something like this:

Someone in Israel has gotten into trouble; it may be economic need or a slanderous attack or a life-threatening illness. There are many possibilities. The affected person calls on God, lamenting this trouble, crying to God for help. That appeal is reinforced by the promise of a thank-offering in the temple. Then the person receives help; trouble and misery are turned to blessing, evil to good. The petitioner fulfills the vow: at the next great pilgrimage feast, when all Israel assembles in Jerusalem (or, in earlier times, in one of the temple cities), that person celebrates her rescue, the new beginning of existence, in a *tôdā*-liturgy.

We should imagine it this way: first the petitioner brings the promised sacrifice into the temple—bread and a sacrificial animal—as the expression of thanksgiving to God. Then parts of the sacrificed animal are consumed in a thanksgiving meal in an outer court of the Jerusalem temple. The person bringing the sacrifice celebrates with relatives and friends, that is, the social group to which he belongs. During the meal the subject describes the trouble that had befallen him and tells how God rescued him. The recitation in all probability contained model texts, elements, and even whole sections of psalms. Perhaps the person quotes the song of lament he had spoken in his trouble, ending with the promise of a thank-offering.

The company at table adopts the rescued person's thanksgiving as its own, thus showing itself united with the whole People of God because the one who received help experienced it as a part of the help God repeatedly gives to God's people. This link between the rescued individual and the whole people of Israel is formulated at the very beginning of Psalm 22:

> ⁴In you our ancestors trusted;
>   they trusted, and you delivered them.
> ⁵To you they cried, and were saved;
>   in you they trusted, and were not put to shame.

The following is also important: the meal taken in company is not merely a "feed," not just an opportunity to eat one's fill. Nor is it just a chance to sit together, exchange news, and have a good time. It is more than that. This meal creates a new communion with God and one another, because the other participants in the meal rejoice over the story of their friend's or relative's rescue, join in the thanksgiving, and so themselves receive a share in the great thing that has been bestowed on them. The prehistory and course of a *tôdā*-liturgy could hypothetically be imagined this way:

Existence-threatening trouble

Lament to God

Plea for help

Promise of a thank-offering

---

Rescue

---

Sacrifice in the temple

Common meal

Narrative of rescue

Assent of the participants at the meal

It is only against such a background that we can really understand why so many individual songs of lament shift so rapidly to the "we" of all Israel. Moreover, there is no problem in understanding that a psalm about the worst of troubles can shift without transition to thanksgiving for rescue. A whole series of psalms can only be understood if we assume a *tôdā*-liturgy as their background. In this context we may consider another psalm, in this case Psalm 116:

> [1]I love the LORD, because he has heard
>     my voice and my supplications.
> [2]Because he inclined his ear to me,
>     therefore I will call on him as long as I live.
> [3]The snares of death encompassed me;
>     the pangs of Sheol laid hold on me;
>     I suffered distress and anguish.
> [4]Then I called on the name of the LORD:
>     "O LORD, I pray, save my life!"
> [5]Gracious is the LORD, and righteous;
>     our God is merciful.
> [6]The LORD protects the simple;
>     when I was brought low, he saved me.
> [7]Return, O my soul, to your rest,
>     for the LORD has dealt bountifully with you.
> [8]For you have delivered my soul from death,
>     my eyes from tears,
>     my feet from stumbling.
> [9]I walk before the LORD
>     in the land of the living.
> [10]I kept my faith, even when I said,
>     "I am greatly afflicted";
> [11]I said in my consternation,
>     "Everyone is a liar."
> [12]What shall I return to the LORD
>     for all his bounty to me?
> [13]I will lift up the cup of salvation
>     and call on the name of the LORD,
> [14]I will pay my vows to the LORD
>     in the presence of all his people.
> [15]Precious in the sight of the LORD
>     is the death of his faithful ones.

<sup>16</sup>O Lord, I am your servant;
  I am your servant, the child of your serving girl.
  You have loosed my bonds.
<sup>17</sup>I will offer to you a thanksgiving sacrifice
  and call on the name of the Lord.
<sup>18</sup>I will pay my vows to the Lord
  in the presence of all his people,
<sup>19</sup>in the courts of the house of the Lord,
  in your midst, O Jerusalem.
  Praise the Lord!

In Psalm 116 we find nearly all the elements we have already seen. They need not always appear in the linear form of a *tôdā-*liturgy. The psalm can also be shaped by freely borrowing from a ritual thank-offering, yet without the background of such a ritual it would be incomprehensible. So this institutional background sheds light on Psalm 22, which is our primary consideration here. Its life-situation is the *tôdā-*liturgy in which people from Israel tell the story of their rescue to a community assembled for a meal.

## A part of world literature

Psalm 22 is an immediate eruption of lament, trust, petition, and praise and yet at the same time it reflects an institution. Psalm 22 does not belong only to the People of God. It is one of the great immortal texts of world literature. First one must appreciate it as a whole; only then may detailed explanation begin.

> To the leader: according to The Deer of the Dawn. A Psalm of David.
> <sup>1</sup>My God, my God, why have you forsaken me?
>   Why are you so far from helping me, from the words of my
>     groaning?
> <sup>2</sup>O my God, I cry by day, but you do not answer;
>   and by night, but find no rest.
> <sup>3</sup>Yet you are holy,
>   enthroned on the praises of Israel.
> <sup>4</sup>In you our ancestors trusted;
>   they trusted, and you delivered them.

⁵To you they cried, and were saved;
    in you they trusted, and were not put to shame.
⁶But I am a worm, and not human;
    scorned by others, and despised by the people.
⁷All who see me mock at me;
    they make mouths at me, they shake their heads;
⁸"Commit your cause to the Lord; let him deliver—
    let him rescue the one in whom he delights!"
⁹Yet it was you who took me from the womb;
    you kept me safe on my mother's breast.
¹⁰On you I was cast from my birth,
    and since my mother bore me you have been my God.
¹¹Do not be far from me,
        for trouble is near
    and there is no one to help.
¹²Many bulls encircle me,
    strong bulls of Bashan surround me;
¹³they open wide their mouths at me,
    like a ravening and roaring lion.
¹⁴I am poured out like water,
    and all my bones are out of joint;
my heart is like wax;
    it is melted within my breast;
¹⁵my mouth is dried up like a potsherd,
    and my tongue sticks to my jaws;
    you lay me in the dust of death.
¹⁶For dogs are all around me;
    a company of evildoers encircles me.
My hands and feet have shriveled;
¹⁷I can count all my bones.
They stare and gloat over me;
¹⁸they divide my clothes among themselves,
    and for my clothing they cast lots.
¹⁹But you, O Lord, do not be far away!
    O my help, come quickly to my aid!
²⁰Deliver my soul from the sword,
    my life from the power of the dog!
²¹Save me from the mouth of the lion!
From the horns of the wild oxen you have rescued me.
²²I will tell of your name to my brothers and sisters;
    in the midst of the congregation I will praise you:

²³You who fear the LORD, praise him!
  All you offspring of Jacob, glorify him;
  stand in awe of him, all you offspring of Israel!
²⁴For he did not despise or abhor
  the affliction of the afflicted;
he did not hide his face from me,
  but heard when I cried to him.
²⁵From you comes my praise in the great congregation;
  my vows I will pay before those who fear him.
²⁶The poor shall eat and be satisfied;
  those who seek him shall praise the LORD.
  May your hearts live forever!
²⁷All the ends of the earth shall remember
  and turn to the LORD;
and all the families of the nations
  shall worship before him.
²⁸For dominion belongs to the LORD,
  and he rules over the nations.
²⁹To him, indeed, shall all who sleep in the earth bow down;
  before him shall bow all who go down to the dust,
  and I shall live for him.
³⁰Posterity will serve him;
  future generations will be told about the Lord,
³¹and proclaim his deliverance to a people yet unborn,
  saying that he has done it.

## Retrospect: the lament

Psalm 22 does not begin with a plea to be heard or a statement of
trust in God. It breaks forth directly in grievous lament:

¹My God, my God, why have you forsaken me?
  Why are you so far from helping me, from the words of my
    groaning?
²O my God, I cry by day, but you do not answer;
  and by night, but find no rest.

The question "why?"—the primeval human question—thus
shapes the beginning of the psalm. Of course, most people only

ask, "Why did this happen to me?" Believers, on the other hand, and the supplicant in Psalm 22 ask: "Why doesn't God help; after all, God is our own and has promised to be close to this people?"

Yet God gives no answer. God is silent. God remains hidden. This crisis, the fact that God is silent, is so beyond measure that orderly, calm speech is impossible. The supplicant cries out to God, laments unceasingly day and night. God does not answer. But then the lament is suddenly interrupted:

> ³Yet you are holy,
>     enthroned on the praises of Israel.
> ⁴In you our ancestors trusted;
>     they trusted, and you delivered them.
> ⁵To you they cried, and were saved;
>     in you they trusted, and were not put to shame.

The petitioner clings to the knowledge that God helped this people in the past. When earlier generations trusted in God, they were not disappointed. When Israel's ancestors cried out to God, God rescued them. Will God not also deliver now—as always in the past?

The interruption to the lament, invoking the past, is introduced by the confession, "Yet you are holy [or: the Holy One]," implying still more: you are the incomprehensible, the Wholly Other whose actions we cannot measure, whose plans we cannot comprehend. Despite all troubles, then, the petitioner clings to her confession of the God of Israel and even expands it: "[You are] enthroned on the praises of Israel."

In Solomon's temple the ark of the covenant was imagined as God's throne; more precisely, the throne is the cherubim carved in the lid of the ark. "Enthroned upon the cherubim" is a fixed formula in the Old Testament (1 Sam 4:4; 2 Sam 6:2; Ps 80:2). That formula, that address, has been reshaped in Psalm 22 and given greater theological depth: God is enthroned "upon the praises of Israel." And yet the psalm continues:

> ⁶But I am a worm, and not human;
>     scorned by others, and despised by the people.
> ⁷All who see me mock at me;
>     they make mouths at me, they shake their heads;

8"Commit your cause to the LORD; let him deliver—
let him rescue the one in whom he delights!"

So the lament breaks forth again. The supplicant's situation remains open. What has made him a "worm," an "unperson," the opposite of the royal human being spoken of in Psalm 8? Is it illness that has derailed him? In the Old Testament health and beauty are among the visible signs of divine blessing. In pagan antiquity physical beauty and striking height were regarded as epiphanies of the divine. Sickness, on the other hand, and a body disabled by illness were often seen as divine punishment. People turned away from unattractive and disgusting individuals. They were avoided, mocked, shoved, and beaten.

So is this text speaking of someone gravely ill who for that very reason is excluded from the society of the sound? The psalm says nothing definite. We always have to reckon with the possibility that images of fatal illness are really meant to portray extreme trouble and persecution. In any case the petitioner is surrounded by mockers and enemies. They show her no pity; she encounters only shunning and ridicule. What is so dreadful is that it is precisely her trust in God and her absolute reliance on God that are being derided. The enemies' speech is saturated with irony and profound sarcasm. We hear a chorus of voices:

8"Commit your cause to the LORD; let him deliver—
let him rescue the one in whom he delights!"

So the opponents are people from Israel. The People of God can direct ridicule and hatred at one who has expected everything from God and has clung to the Lord. The fact that the supplicant's enemies come from Israel itself is the worst of the worst. But then the direction of speech shifts again:

9Yet it was you who took me from the womb;
you kept me safe on my mother's breast.
10On you I was cast from my birth,
and since my mother bore me you have been my God.
11Do not be far from me,
for trouble is near
and there is no one to help.

Against all the hostility the petitioner again expresses trust in God, looking back on his own life. In a daring image he appeals to God as midwife: it was God who took the supplicant from his mother's womb and laid him on the maternal breast.

On God she has been cast "from my birth." That existentialist-sounding statement presumes a particular legal custom: the newborn was laid on the father's knee; the father thereby recognized it as his own legitimate child. Our passage thus says that God is the petitioner's father, has accepted her as his own child and guided her throughout her life. The supplicant now reminds God of that, reminding herself as well. In the throes of death people often call for their mother or father: so here the one who prays Psalm 22. There is no more help in anyone, only in God. In the next verses the lament again breaks through:

> ¹²Many bulls encircle me,
>   strong bulls [or: oxen] of Bashan surround me;
> ¹³they open wide their mouths at me,
>   like a ravening and roaring lion.

The opponents are compared with beasts: bulls, oxen, lions, and later, in verse 16, with a pack of hounds. Bashan was an area east of the Jordan. The cattle raised there were considered especially strong and aggressive. But the opponents are not only compared to animals as something dangerous; they are inhuman. So we have a new sequence of images:

> ¹⁴I am poured out like water,
>   and all my bones are out of joint;
> my heart is like wax;
>   it is melted within my breast;
> ¹⁵my mouth is dried up like a potsherd,
>   and my tongue sticks to my jaws;
>   you lay me in the dust of death.

Evidently these are images of the most serious illness: fever, thirst, pains in the limbs, deathly fatigue. But the worst of it all is that it is *God* who has cast the petitioner into the dust of death. The images shift again with verse 16:

<sup>16</sup>For dogs are all around me;
   a company of evildoers encircles me.
My hands and feet have shriveled;
<sup>17</sup>I can count all my bones.
They stare and gloat over me;
<sup>18</sup>they divide my clothes among themselves,
   and for my clothing they cast lots.

Now the enemies appear in the guise of a pack of wild dogs that run yelping through the streets at night. Everyone who has been in the Middle East is familiar with the sleepless nights in which one is repeatedly awakened by hordes of stray dogs that gather around the house or the tent and yelp wildly as they fight over some capture. That is how the supplicant's enemies surround and besiege her.

Then the image of animals is abandoned again and we see only human enemies surrounding the defenseless victim. They tie his hands and feet and gloat over his suffering. They treat him like someone already dead; they seize his belongings and divide his meager possessions.

The swiftly succeeding images of illness, persecution, and near death deepen the impression that this is not about just any kind of trouble. Instead, the fate of the petitioner becomes the archetypical image of the primeval suffering of genuine believers in Israel. Next the lament reverses the petition again, accompanying it with a statement of trust: "O my help!"

<sup>19</sup>But you, O Lord, do not be far away!
   O my help, come quickly to my aid!
<sup>20</sup>Deliver my soul from the sword,
   my life from the power of the dog!
<sup>21a</sup>Save me from the mouth of the lion!
<sup>21b</sup>From the horns of the wild oxen

Verses 20 and 21 and their repeated images of trouble summarize everything that has gone before: the paws of the dogs, the mouth of the lion, the horns of the oxen. Added to these we see the drawn sword. Now it is only about naked survival.

## The present time: the meal

This is the precise turning point in the psalm, the utterly decisive watershed. With reference back to the beginning of the psalm, where it was said that God is silent and gives the petitioner no answer, now we read: "You have rescued me." That means the supplicant has been heard.

> <sup>21c</sup>you have rescued me.
> <sup>22</sup>I will tell of your name to my brothers and sisters;
>     in the midst of the congregation I will praise you:
> <sup>23</sup>You who fear the LORD, praise him!
>     All you offspring of Jacob, glorify him;
>     stand in awe of him, all you offspring of Israel!
> <sup>24</sup>For he did not despise or abhor
>     the affliction of the afflicted;
> he did not hide his face from me,
>     but heard when I cried to him.
> <sup>25</sup>From you comes my praise in the great congregation;
>     my vows I will pay before those who fear him.
> <sup>26</sup>The poor shall eat and be satisfied;
>     those who seek him shall praise the LORD.
>     "May your hearts live forever!"

It is clear that these verses describe a new scenario. Now we hear again and again that God has heard the petitioner ("he did not despise or abhor the affliction of the afflicted"), that he is in the process of fulfilling his vow ("my vows I will pay before those who fear him"), that he has gathered his siblings around him ("I will tell of your name to my brothers and sisters"), that a meal is in progress ("The poor shall eat and be satisfied"), and that the rescued one will relate, in the course of this meal, how God delivered him ("in the midst of the congregation I will praise you").

Because the psalm speaks of the rescued person's testimony before "brothers and sisters" we could certainly think also of the physical family, one's own clan. But that would not be enough, for in verse 23 the psalm speaks of the "offspring of Jacob" and the "offspring of Israel," and in verse 25 of the "great congregation." Thus all Israel comes into view—or would it be better to say the true Israel, for we have seen that the petitioner's enemies themselves come from Israel, and besides, the psalm speaks in this very context of the "poor" (v. 26) and those "who fear God" (v. 25).

Thus the psalm supposes a real assembly and yet envisions all the God-fearing people in Israel together with it: all the poor (that is, all who trust in God, in humility and fidelity). We could also say that the "poor" are stricken and humbled Israel, clinging to its God and not ceasing to sing God's praise. The petitioner's "I"—as in many of the psalms—is thus at the same time Israel's "I." The little assembly at the *tôdā*-liturgy expands to form a gathering of the true, eschatological Israel.

## The future: the banquet of the nations

Then, in the last part of the psalm, the view expands yet again: from the present to the future and from Israel to include the whole world. There are echoes of the motifs of the pilgrimage of nations to Zion and the eschatological meal of the peoples before God. The day is coming when the true Israel will shine before all nations and enlighten them. Then the peoples will turn to the Lord and join in the praise uttered by the People of God:

> ²⁷All the ends of the earth shall remember
>     and turn to the LORD;
> and all the families of the nations
>     shall worship before him.
> ²⁸For dominion belongs to the LORD,
>     and he rules over the nations.
> ²⁹To him, indeed, shall all who sleep in the earth bow down;
>     before him shall bow all who go down to the dust,
>     and I shall live for him.
> ³⁰Posterity will serve him;
>     future generations will be told about the Lord,
> ³¹and proclaim his deliverance to a people yet unborn,
>     saying that he has done it.

In verse 29 the view expands to include even the underworld, the house of the dead: those very dead will worship God on that day. Thus the psalm closes with an immense finale. The supplicant's personal thanks have expanded to encompass the eschatological rejoicing of the nations because of their salvation. What this text only alludes to is broadly described in Isaiah 25:6-8:

> On this mountain the LORD of hosts will make for all peoples
>     a feast of rich food, a feast of well-aged wines,
>         of rich food filled with marrow, of well-aged wines strained
>             clear.
> And he will destroy on this mountain
>     the shroud that is cast over all peoples,
>     the sheet that is spread over all nations;
>     he will swallow up death forever.
> Then the Lord GOD will wipe away the tears from all faces,
>     and the disgrace of his people he will take away from all the
>         earth,
>     for the LORD has spoken.

Because in the end all the nations will assemble before God, Psalm 22:29 even expands the praise of God to include the dead in the underworld. In doing so the psalm contradicts Israel's ancient maxim that the dead cannot praise God. It may be that a traditionalist-thinking copyist therefore inserted a dogmatic correction into the original text in verse 30: one who is dead can no longer serve God, but her posterity can.

## Jesus' dying prayer

Christians can never pray Psalm 22 without thinking of Jesus' death, because the death-crisis depicted in the psalm came true for Jesus on the cross. More than that: there is good reason to believe that Jesus prayed this psalm as his dying prayer while hanging on the cross.

Crucifixion was a gruesome method of execution thought up by people who wanted to torture others. For the Romans crucifixion was so horrible and dishonorable that it could only be imposed on slaves and non-Romans. Cicero wrote: "The mere name of the gibbet [= cross] should be far removed, not only from the persons of Roman citizens—from their thoughts, and eyes, and ears" (*Pro Rabirio* 16).

In the Roman Empire the penalty of crucifixion, even for slaves and non-Romans, was clearly limited by law—it could be applied only in cases of serious crime such as murder, robbery of a temple, high treason, and insurrection—because the death struggles of the crucified usually lasted a long time, far more than the hours Jesus hung on the cross (six hours if one follows Mark 15:25, 34; only three hours according to John 19:14). The inhuman brutality of crucifixion lay especially in the fact that its aim was a slow, drawn-out death. In most cases the ultimate cause of death must have been circulatory failure. That was because a crucified person—unless a wooden block was provided as a kind of seat—hung by the arms, which had to sustain the full weight of the body. That led in a very short time to severe arterial blockage and inability to breathe. Then the crucified, quite without willing it, lifted his or her body upward, which exacerbated the wounds in the feet. As soon as exhaustion led to the body's sinking, the hideous cycle of self-raising and collapse began all over again. Because the feet were nailed in place and so supported the body at least from time to time, the death-struggle of a crucified person often lasted all day. If their executioners wanted them dead, they broke their legs. Then the whole weight of the body hung from the arms, and death followed quickly as circulation ceased.

It was in that gruesome situation of hanging on the cross that Jesus prayed Psalm 22, or at least began to recite it. He probably knew it by heart. At that time there were quite a few people in Israel who could pray the whole psalm by heart. According to Mark, Jesus cried out at the ninth hour—about three o'clock in the afternoon—in a loud voice: " 'Eloi, Eloi, lema sabachthani?' which means, 'My God, my God, why have you forsaken me?' " (Mark 15:34). That is the beginning of Psalm 22, and it represents the whole psalm. But it could be that Jesus recited the whole psalm as his dying prayer. Support for that is found in the observation that some of those standing nearby said "Listen, he is calling for Elijah" (15:35). That was probably a misunderstanding, a mishearing. But how could it have come about?

There is a simple explanation. Psalm 22:10 reads, "since my mother bore me you have been my God." "You are/have been my God" in the original Hebrew text was *eli attā*, literally "my God, you." That *eli attā* could have been heard as *Eliyya tā*, "Elijah, come [to my aid]!" Pious Jews were accustomed to call on the prophet Elijah as a helper when they were in serious trouble. So there was a misunderstanding, but we can see from it that Jesus probably spoke the whole psalm and that he recited it aloud. As we have said, in antiquity scarcely anyone prayed silently.

## Why Psalm 22?

Why does Jesus, on the cross, cry out at least the beginning of the twenty-second psalm, if not the whole of it, and so identify this prayer with his own dying situation? "My God, my God, why have you forsaken me?" is most certainly not a cry of despair, as is sometimes asserted. But it is a cry of the utmost abandonment, and Jesus felt that abandonment.

The council had ordered his death, accusing him before the Roman procurator as a political insurrectionist, and had used every means to bring about his execution. Jesus had fallen between the millstones of two powers much more mighty than he, authorities who did not want to deal with the question of truth or who saw it as their religious obligation to get him out of sight. On the whole Jesus had not found many hearers in Israel. When he was condemned to crucifixion most of Jerusalem was probably asleep.

Moreover, Jesus knew Deuteronomy 21:23: "anyone hung on a tree is under God's curse," that is, forever abandoned by God. Did Jesus feel abandoned by God? Here we are approaching a limit where all-too-facile answers fail us and we must fall silent. We can only say that the psalm Jesus prayed or, by crying out its opening words, made altogether his own, contains both: that God is silent and yet that God answers; God's awful hiddenness and the showing of God's face (cp. v. 24); the lostness of the supplicant but also unshakeable trust; final loneliness and the new gift of community.

Did Jesus guess that it would be his death itself that would create new praise in the midst of Israel? Did he know that his execution would assemble Israel anew, that it would be salvation for the "many" after God had rescued him from death? Words from the Last Supper affirm this clearly:

> This is my blood of the covenant, which is poured out for many. Truly I tell you, I will never again drink of the fruit of the vine until that day when I drink it new in the kingdom of God. (Mark 14:24-25)

There could be no more suitable prayer for Jesus than Psalm 22, which was able to interpret his death as God's action in him, in Israel, and for the world. Seen in retrospect Psalm 22 summarizes everything Christians celebrate in Holy Week and the fifty days of Easter: in this psalm, on Good Friday, they share in the death-struggle of one who is persecuted and ridiculed. On Holy Saturday they hear how eschatological salvation reaches even the dead in the underworld. On Easter they experience the rescue of the despised victim from the crisis of death. Finally, at Pentecost, they celebrate how his rescue and the telling of it creates community. Psalm 22 reflects the whole liturgy of the passion and of Easter from Good Friday to Easter morning, and even to Pentecost.

It is also true that Psalm 22 reflects something of the lives of those who pray it: loneliness, distance from God, separation—but also rescue and a new togetherness in faith.

## Chapter 7

# The Psalms Give Us a Home

### Riding the streetcar

What is home? I was born in Frankfurt am Main and lived there for twenty-five years. I sometimes go back there for a few days because I feel homesick, even though I have no desire to live in that peculiar city again. What is the source of the magic that still works on me? Is it the river with its bridges, the ancient imperial cathedral, the last remains of the old city? Is it the streets of my childhood, the parks where we played, the yellow sand of the gravel quarry, the blue Taunus hills? Or is it the friends and relatives who still live there? It is all of that, and yet it is not. Above all it is the language, the local dialect. I ride the streetcar for hours to see the well-known parts of the city but above all to listen to the people talk. There is something special about the language of childhood days that warms us and gives us life. It is home.

No one can say that in our faith life we have no need of a home. Our home is in the churches, the beautiful ones and even the hideous ones; it is in the liturgical colors, the gestures of worship, the church year with its festivals, the old and new songs. It is, above all, the language of the liturgy, of the collects, the psalms, the eucharistic prayer.

Naturally when I say "language" I am not speaking of Latin or German or English. I mean what speaks to us through Latin or German or English. I am talking about the sound, the melody of speech, the images, the meaning. In that sense the language of liturgy is a language all its own. It is not street language, media jargon, or the formulas of science. We really must not be ashamed of this special language. It has its own necessity, its own right, its own dignity. For believers the language of worship is itself a little piece of home.

Obviously the language of our prayers and hymns can go awry. It can be phony or unfeeling. It can be debased, heard wrongly, cloying, sentimental, awkward, watered-down, or ridden into the ground. Then it is no longer a home; it is a cheap substitute that tries to pander to us. God preserve us from "happy-clappy songs."

But from the beginning the church has possessed an antidote to whatever might infect liturgical language, and that is the Psalter. It was not only a constant corrective. It not only renewed the church's praying and singing again and again. The Psalter was home, and so it will always be.

## Our mouth filled with laughter

What makes the language of the Psalms so irreplaceable? To begin with, the Psalms have nothing shapeless or vague about them. They do not run riot. They are composed; they have clear contours. It is true that there are many repetitions in the structure of individual psalms and of the Psalter itself, but oddly enough these do not diffuse the language of the psalms; they intensify it all the more. They internalize and deepen it. Thus Psalm 136 repeats the same antiphon in every verse, like a litany:

> O give thanks to the LORD, for he is good,
>     for his steadfast love endures forever.
> O give thanks to the God of gods,
>     for his steadfast love endures forever.
> O give thanks to the Lord of lords,
>     for his steadfast love endures forever;
> who alone does great wonders,
>     for his steadfast love endures forever. (Ps 136:1-4)

And so it continues through Israel's history. It doesn't put us to sleep, but it lets the praying person rest—in the dependability and fidelity of God. But the Psalter has another equally effective technique of repetition in its constant parallelisms, frequently even so-called *synonymous* parallelisms. They repeat what has been said in new terms, for example, in Psalm 126:

> When the LORD restored the fortunes of Zion,
>     we were like those who dream.
> Then our mouth was filled with laughter,
>     and our tongue with shouts of joy. (Ps 126:1-2)

Mouth and tongue have the same meaning, as do laughter and joy, but their unequal weight makes the statement more effective. The laughter continues and even becomes a shout of joy. Psalm 124 contains a synonymous parallelism in three stages:

> if it had not been the LORD who was on our side,
>     when our enemies attacked us . . .
> then the flood would have swept us away,
>     the torrent would have gone over us;
> then over us would have gone
>     the raging waters. (Ps 124:2, 4-5)

In the Judean desert sudden rainstorms can turn narrow valleys used as roads into deathtraps in no time at all. In Psalm 124 that phenomenon is described in three variations: flood waters, a gushing torrent, raging waters. In the first place this is a natural phenomenon experienced over and over again, but behind such a natural occurrence the people of that time sensed something more dreadful: the chaotic powers of history that devour whole nations. That power of chaos is depicted in the threefold characterization. Language needs space in order to come to terms with the monstrous phenomenon in view here. But the repetition need not always be synonymous, as it is here; it can also be *antithetical*, that is, structured as contrast:

> The LORD lifts up the downtrodden;
>     he casts the wicked to the ground. (Ps 147:6)

We should not rush to spiritualize such images; rather, we should start by visualizing them in all their power: the "poor," that is, those who are already bowed down, those who are weighed down and can no longer stand upright—it is precisely these whom God helps to stand; it is God who lifts up their heads. In contrast those who shamelessly desire evil, the exploiters who do violence to the poor: these are they whom God presses to the ground, putting them in the very position formerly forced on the poor and disenfranchised. Here, as in the *Magnificat*, we are talking about revolution. Here is yet another example of antithetical parallelism:

> Weeping may linger for the night,
>   but joy comes with the morning. (Ps 30:5)

Night and morning, weeping and jubilation are sharply contrasted here. In the evening a laborer in ancient Israel was not only dead tired; all the day's troubles would have added up. Hopelessness began to rise. The psalm expresses all that in a single word: weeping. But in the morning all was changed. Morning was seen as the time of God's saving intervention. Joy replaces weeping.

The switch between day and night is very different in Psalm 19: here the subject is the ongoing praise sung by the whole universe:

> The heavens are telling the glory of God,
>   and the firmament proclaims his handiwork.
> Day to day pours forth speech,
>   and night to night declares knowledge. (Ps 19:1-2)

The synonymous parallelism of heaven and firmament is followed by an antithetical counterpart: day and night. But here the antithesis represents the uninterrupted praise of God. The sequence of days and nights is like a relay: praise is handed on from runner to runner.

There are also numerous so-called *synthetic* parallelisms. They develop an uttered thought while retaining the same keyword or keeping to the same visual field:

> See how [the wicked] conceive evil,
>   and are pregnant with mischief,
>   and bring forth lies. (Ps 7:14)

So we see the conception, gestation, and birth of evil. First it is conceived—by others. Then they bear it within them for a long time. It grows, stirs, begins to kick; at some point or other it inevitably emerges. Then the evil is in the world; it cries out and one day it will beget progeny. So the visual of "deceit / injustice / evil" remains, only with variations. The progress lies in the "conception / pregnancy / birth."

## By the rivers of Babylon

The technique of repetition is often applied much more subtly, however, than in the examples given above. It can link two successive psalms or a whole series of them by means of repeated words or themes, thus making one psalm interpret the other. Psalm 137, for example, begins by considering the deportees from Israel who were enslaved in Mesopotamia, being forced to do such slave tasks as clearing irrigation canals clogged with sand or weeds:

> ¹By the rivers of Babylon—
>     there we sat down and there we wept
>     when we remembered Zion.
> ²On the willows there
>     we hung up our harps.
> ³For there our captors
>     asked us for songs,
> and our tormentors asked for mirth, saying,
>     "Sing us one of the songs of Zion!"
> ⁴How could we sing the LORD's song
>     in a foreign land?

The psalm ends by hoping for divine judgment on and punishment of Babylon. Its conclusion is so shocking that many Christians think they can no longer pray it. Pope Paul VI struck it from the breviary:

> ⁸Happy shall they be who pay you back
>     what you have done to us!
> ⁹Happy shall they be who take your little ones
>     and dash them against the rock!

That describes the way war was conducted in those times, but it is really dreadful. How can a text like that be a home for us? Careful! The Psalter is neither a handbook of moral theology nor advice literature with rules for behavior and civility. It expresses every human emotion: rage, fury, fear, shuddering, sighing, longing, trust, jubilation, delight. The Psalter is a book of powerful emotions. It suppresses nothing that moves within the human heart.

There is no question that we harbor anger against injustices we have suffered, an immeasurable desire for justice, longing that a painful past may be made good. The real question is what we do with the rage and bitterness when they arise in us. Here Psalm 138, following after Psalm 137, gives an astonishing answer. As its superscription says, it is a psalm "of David." That is: the editors or redactors of the Psalter intend that we should read it as a psalm from David or, in other words, from the mouth of the Messiah.

This psalm of David is linked to Psalm 137. The keyword "sing" in Psalm 137 is recalled and repeated in Psalm 138:5, and the whole theme of Psalm 137 is presented all over again: the banished do not want to sing Yhwh-songs "in a foreign land," the home of other gods. But now the coming Messiah says to God:

> I give you thanks, O Lord, with my whole heart;
>    before the gods I sing your praise;
> I bow down toward your holy temple
>    and give thanks to your name for your steadfast love and your
>       faithfulness. (Ps 138:1-2)

This means that Psalm 138 is the antithesis of Psalm 137. The *Messiah* has no problem making music and singing songs of Zion even in a hostile land, in the face of the foreign gods—and *with him* the deportees themselves no longer hesitate. They simply sing their songs in the direction of Jerusalem. And how is that possible? It is so because history has moved on. The situation has changed; the people, together with their rulers, have turned to the God of Israel:

> All the kings of the earth shall praise you, O Lord,
>    for they have heard the words of your mouth.
> They shall sing of the ways of the Lord,
>    for great is the glory of the Lord. (Ps 138:4-5)

That is not yet present; it is still a vision, but it expresses an enormous hope, and that hope itself changes everything. It gives inner freedom to praise the Lord, even in a foreign land. The hope for vengeance on Babylon and its children has fallen silent and no longer plays any part. Suddenly the oppressors are seen with new eyes. There is to be hope for them as well. How foolish it is to destroy such a conversation between the psalms by simply erasing an essential part of it!

So Psalm 138 is in dialogue with Psalm 137. It does not wipe away its trouble; that has to be spoken of. But it gives a completely new solution in which there is no longer room for violence and revenge. That new solution contains an unending, confident hope for the world's violent history. Could it be that praying in that way might bring us home?

## Escape to Israel's God

We wanted to look more closely at the "language" of the Psalms. That obviously includes considering the poetic techniques employed by the authors of the Psalter. We have seen some of those techniques, but the language of the Psalter also includes the images and metaphors we encounter in the 150 psalms. We can say without exaggeration that the Psalter is bulging with images. Of course, they all come from the world of that time, from the authors' surroundings. The fact that those images can still frighten or delight us speaks for their power.

In Psalm 16 a person confesses how she has turned away from the gods of the land even though they still shower her with sinister suggestions. She flees from her ancient gods to the God of Israel and tells Yhwh, "I have no good apart from you" (v. 3). The psalm continues:

> their drink offerings of blood I will not pour out
> or take their names upon my lips.
> The Lord is my chosen portion and my cup;
> you hold my lot.
> The boundary lines have fallen for me in pleasant places;
> I have a goodly heritage. (Ps 16:4-6)

Blood sacrifice, cup, lot, portion, boundary lines—all those things are at first strange to us. In pagan sacrifices blood was sprinkled on the earth; cup, lot, and boundary lines are associated with the processes of land distribution in Israel. So at first glance these are distant worlds! And yet . . . we know exactly what it means to cease taking part in the search for ecstatic experience in the rituals of our neo-pagan society, just as seductive as the ancient cult of Ba'al, and to seek our portion of joy with the true God alone. Then all at once a new "land" filled with promise can open up to us. It may be that Psalm 30 will come true for us:

> You have turned my mourning into dancing;
>     you have taken off my sackcloth
>     and clothed me with joy,
> so that my soul may praise you and not be silent.
>     O LORD my God, I will give thanks to you forever. (Ps 30:11-12)

We have long since abandoned the wearing of mourning clothes. They were rough, coarse, and basically dirty sacks. The old mourning rituals (matted hair, dirt on the face, ragged fingernails) are also things of the past. Nevertheless, we are at home with this language. We have experienced how God can clothe us with joy and protects us "like the apple of the eye" (Ps 17:8), that God "crown[s] the year with . . . bounty" (Ps 65:11) and shelters us "in the shadow of [God's] wings" (Ps 17:8).

## Enemies, the wicked, and persecutors

The images in the Psalter become especially dramatic when they represent the supplicant's enemies, the violent and godless: "violence covers them like a garment" (Ps 73:6); "there is wrong in [their] hands" (cp. Ps 7:3); "pride is their necklace" (Ps 73:6); "[they] are plotting destruction" and "[their] tongue is like a sharp razor" (Ps 52:1-2); they speak with "speech smoother than butter" (Ps 55:22) but "their throats are open graves" (Ps 5:9). "They lurk in secret like a lion in its covert; they lurk that they may seize the poor" (Ps 10:9); "[they] eat up my people as they eat bread" (Ps

53:4). But their end matches their behavior: "Death shall be their shepherd" (Ps 49:14); "like sheep they are appointed for Sheol" (Ps 49:14), "[they] are like chaff that the wind drives away" (Ps 1:4), "the way of the wicked will perish" (Ps 1:6).

Nowhere in the Psalter is the language more vivid than when it speaks of enemies—and the Psalter talks of them incessantly. The book of Psalms has its own rich vocabulary: it calls them opponents, the godless, wicked, sinners, evildoers, persecutors, besiegers, oppressors, mockers, the proud, schemers, liars, betrayers, murderers, men of blood, the violent. They appear in nearly every psalm, even where we would least expect them.

What is going on here? Did the composers of the psalms suffer from a persecution complex or a neurotic fear of enemies? Did they live in some state of insanity that sees persecutors emerging from every crack? Certainly not! We have to keep in mind that ridiculous little Israel was threatened, historically, almost without respite by great powers: Egypt, Assyria, later Babylon, the Seleucids, and finally the Romans.

Besides, it is by no means always about external enemies. In most cases the opponents come from within Israel itself, as in Psalm 12, for example:

> Help, O Lord, for there is no longer anyone who is godly;
>     the faithful have disappeared from humankind.
> They utter lies to each other;
>     with flattering lips and a double heart they speak.
> May the Lord cut off all flattering lips,
>     the tongue that makes great boasts,
> those who say, "With our tongues we will prevail;
>     our lips are our own—who is our master?"
> "Because the poor are despoiled, because the needy groan,
>     I will now rise up," says the Lord;
> "I will place them in the safety for which they long." (Ps 12:1-5)

Here corrupt relationships within the People of God itself are attacked. The socially weak are oppressed and robbed; every escape route is closed to the poor. It seems there is a social class in Israel that makes everything permissible for its members:

> They flatter and lie "with smooth lips." And above all: they proceed ruthlessly in legal matters and contractual relationships. They promise everything and stop at nothing. They stage legal procedures that they decide in their own favor through false-hoods and perjury. They eliminate anyone who stands in their way because they have the power and the "right connections." And because they apparently succeed in everything they con-sider themselves the measure of all things: "who is our master?" (Erich Zenger)[1]

We have to reckon with that kind of background for many of the psalms; nor should we forget that in Israel there was a social consciousness that had been sensitized by the prophets. Believers within the People of God could no longer accept the rape of the poor and abuse of the weak. Israel was oriented toward mutual solidarity, truthfulness, right, and fidelity. The fact that the psalms repeatedly complain against the wicked, the oppressors, and the scoffers has nothing to do with some deviant enemy-complex but rather with a honed knowledge of what Israel was supposed to be within God's plan.

That knowledge was kept alive by particular groups whose concern was the true Israel willed by God. Among them a Psalms-piety must have played a prominent role, and it was precisely those groups who were attacked, vilified, and excluded.

Consequently one who prays the psalms today may not react by saying: for heaven's sake, why these continual images of enmity? Instead we should ask: do I myself act on behalf of the kind of togetherness the Psalms long for, one in which the poor, the op-pressed, the persecuted brothers and sisters in the People of God receive help?

But in this context we always have to keep in mind also how the psalms raise their voice against the godless and the violent. They do not call for hatred or counterviolence and most certainly not for terrorism. They cry to God. They call on God as the savior and protector of the poor. They deliberately refuse any personal

---

1. Erich Zenger, *Psalmen. Auslegungen. 1. Mit meinem Gott überspringe ich Mauern* (Freiburg: Herder, 2nd ed. 2006), 179. Cp. Erich Zenger, *A God of Vengeance?*, trans. Linda M. Maloney (Louisville: Westminster John Knox, 1994), 79.

application of violence. They beg God to judge the opponents—
but in this connection judgment means restoration of the right:
rights for the poor and weak, restoration of justice, clarification of
what human beings cannot clarify, the restoration of truth. In this
sense, too, the Psalms can be a home for us. I, at any rate, do not
want to live in a society in which truth is constantly manipulated
and justice is trodden underfoot. The Psalter desires justice and
truth; it calls for support of the suffering and the poor. I long for
the society it proposes.

## Invitation to a banquet

Perhaps now we can better understand why the subject of enemies
and oppressors appears everywhere in the Psalms and in fact must
be there. It runs through even what may be the most beautiful text
in the whole Psalter, Psalm 23:

> ¹The LORD is my shepherd, I shall not want.
>   ²He makes me lie down in green pastures;
> he leads me beside still waters;
>   ³he restores my soul.
> He leads me in right paths
>   for his name's sake.
> ⁴Even though I walk through the darkest valley,
>   I fear no evil;
> for you are with me;
>   your rod and your staff—
>   they comfort me.
> ⁵You prepare a table before me
>   in the presence of my enemies;
> you anoint my head with oil;
>   my cup overflows.
> ⁶Surely goodness and mercy shall follow me
>   all the days of my life,
> and I shall dwell in the house of the LORD
>   my whole life long.

Psalm 23 is one of the best-loved of all the psalms, and rightly
so. But why does this psalm in particular have such an appeal for

us? It is probably because of the beauty and poetic consistency of its imagery, combined with the assurance of absolute security that runs throughout the psalm.

The first field of imagery is that of shepherds or, more precisely, that of semi-nomads who, while they have a fixed abode, travel through part of the year together with their flocks, from pasture to pasture. It rains even in the desert, but the particular localities where it rains and then, within a few days, everything is green are few and far between. One must know where they are at a particular time. God knows, and God leads the wanderers to the perfect places within the desiccated land.

The shepherds' world has always played a considerable role in literature. When poets contemplated the pastoral scene they quickly turned to bucolic images of gamboling sheep and a sentimental "back to nature" mood. But Psalm 23 is far removed from such attitudes. Instead, it falls within the shepherd metaphors of the Near Eastern ideology of rulers. In that time and place the kings always liked to be depicted as shepherds who guarded and protected their people.

That is precisely the point at which the psalm begins. The point of its first line is not that YHWH is lauded as a *shepherd* but that those praying the psalm confess YHWH as their own shepherd. The meaning is: "*My* shepherd is YHWH and no one else." That is, there are gods one ought to have nothing to do with, and there are royal shepherds to whom one had better not entrust oneself. "[They] lord it over [their people]; and those in authority . . . are called benefactors" (Luke 22:25).

Those praying this psalm know that it is different with YHWH: those who have YHWH as their shepherd will lack nothing. They will be led where rain has fallen and the steppe has grown green overnight. They will be led to where there are springs that have not yet dried up and where the flock can drink without haste and lie down to rest. Even the path through deeply carved, steep canyons where animals could slip or where traps have been set causes no concern in the presence of this shepherd.

With verse 5 the visual field changes. Now those praying are no longer among the protected flock who walk behind their shepherd; they are guests at a banquet. They have been invited by YHWH, who honors them by welcoming them into his house. That honor will protect them in the future against all who are hostile and envious. They can eat in peace in the face of the malevolent looks of their enemies.

As an additional honor, at the beginning of the meal the host has anointed their heads with perfume ("oil": at that time perfume had an oil base) and has gone to the length of setting the table for them and handing them overflowing cups.

In the last part of the psalm even that image is surpassed: "Surely goodness and mercy shall follow me all the days of my life." Now it is not enemies who pursue; instead, it is the grace of God. And those who pray the psalm are not only guests at a banquet but residents in the home of the host: "I shall dwell in the house of the LORD my whole life long." The banqueting house has been transformed into the temple of God.

It is possible that "my whole life long" (lit.: "for length of days") means a time that has no end (thus the Authorized Version's "forever" that is so familiar to English speakers). The Psalms very often play with the idea of a life beyond death without speaking of it in clear terms.

## The "I" of Israel

Thus far I have regularly spoken of "the supplicant" or "the one praying" the psalm: after all, it speaks in the "I" form throughout. But who is this "I"? A modern person naturally thinks of the self, the individual, a single person. But is that right? If we read Psalm 23 more closely we see that there is a nearly constant reference to the history of Israel. The God who leads Israel like a flock is a fixed and familiar image. Compare, for example, Psalm 78:52-54:

> Then he led out his people like sheep,
>     and guided them in the wilderness like a flock.
> He led them in safety, so that they were not afraid;
>     but the sea overwhelmed their enemies.
> And he brought them to his holy hill,
>     to the mountain that his right hand had won.

Clearly, Psalm 23 is not telling a story merely of an individual's being led; it is also about the divine accompaniment that all Israel experiences. For example, being led to restful places beside water alludes to the story of the Wilderness Wandering: God provided this people with water from the rock and gave them manna to eat.

Similarly, the concept of "rest" (we would think of relaxing after long effort) is something applied to the whole people. "Rest" is characteristic of the Promised Land. There Israel, after its march through the wilderness, finally finds tranquility (cp., for example, Jer 31:2). Probably when Christians pray that their dead may find "eternal rest" most of them have no idea that the concept originated with the idea of rest in the Land, a finally-having-arrived in the fullness given by God after the long road through the wilderness.

The second visual field in the psalm also alludes to Israel's history. The oil on the head of the guest and the wine in the cup represent the richness of the Promised Land: the oil from its olive trees and the richness of its grapes. Unlike the wilderness generation who rejected God again and again and repeatedly fell back into their old skepticism ("Can God spread a table in the wilderness?" [Ps 78:19]), here Israel says "You prepare a table before me in the presence of my enemies; you anoint my head with oil; my cup overflows."

In Psalm 23, then, it is not just an individual who prays. The "I" (as so often in the Psalms) is also the "I" of Israel—and in this case the "I" of a purified Israel. Here is no longer the unbelieving, doubting, resistant Israel of the wilderness generation who slandered the Land but instead a believing Israel that already sees in faith and is entering into its fulfillment.

## Gentiles on the way to Zion

So who is it who prays Psalm 23? Is it an individual, or is it Israel? Current exegesis has revealed yet a third possibility. Here we see again, as we saw in Psalm 137 ("By the rivers of Babylon"), the quiet revolution in Psalms research. We already saw that many psalms are linked together, one interpreting the others, or how a theme from one psalm will be extended into the next and will be newly illuminated there. What is the textual context of Psalm 23?

Psalm 22 ("My God, my God, why have you forsaken me?") ends, as we saw, with a grand hope: all the ends of the earth return to the Lord. All peoples will revere God. The mighty of the earth will dine before the God of Israel and even the dead will worship this God.

Should Psalm 23 turn away from that universal perspective and speak only about Israel or a single pious person? How could that be, when the pilgrimage of the nations to Zion that dawned on our sight at the end of Psalm 22 has been more fully described in Psalm 23? In that case the speaker of Psalm 23 represents the Gentiles who are on their way to Zion. Let us test whether the psalm functions in that fashion!

"Yhwh is *my* shepherd": that fits perfectly in such a context. Thus the one praying would say, "I no longer trust my old gods but only one, the God of Israel," and would go on to describe the feeling of being led by this God, from watercourse to watercourse but also through dangerous clefts. The speaker would be describing the pilgrimage of the nations but at the same time picturing how to find the true God. The path is a long one, impossible to plan, and dangerous—and yet those wandering between two worlds (that of paganism and that of the true God) are led in safety. Ultimately they arrive, and then begins the feast on Mount Zion as Isaiah had depicted it: "a feast of rich foods, a feast of well-aged wines" (Isa 25:6). The feast would never end. The nations would receive a share in the election of Israel, forever: "they would dwell in the house of the Lord their whole lives long."

The bridge between Psalms 22 and 23 is thus fairly stable. It holds. One can walk on it. But does the path lead onward to Psalm 24? That, we might say, is the ultimate test.

## A ritual at the gate

In its central section (vv. 3-6) Psalm 24 reflects a so-called "ritual entry into the temple." Pilgrims have come to Jerusalem from afar and seek access to the temple complex, but before the gate is opened to them they are asked whether they are worthy. Only if they answer in the affirmative do the double gates open to them. The catechizing begins in verse 3:

> Who shall ascend the hill of the LORD?
>    And who shall stand in his holy place?
> Those who have clean hands and pure hearts,
>    who do not lift up their souls to what is false,
>    and do not swear deceitfully.
> They will receive blessing from the LORD,
>    and vindication from the God of their salvation. (Ps 24:3-5)

When the nations make pilgrimage to Zion, naturally they must also be subjected to this test. The conditions for entry are formulated in Psalm 24 (in contrast to Psalm 15) in such a way that they apply especially to Gentiles: They must have separated themselves from "falsehood" and "deceit," that is, from their false gods. Then they, too, will be subject to the blessing of the LORD, that is, of YHWH. The modification of the conditions for entry confirms what I have said before; in verse 6 comes the final affirmation:

> Such is the company of those who seek him,
>    who seek your face, O Jacob. (Ps 24:6, modified)

In many translations, including the NRSV, the verse reads:

> Such is the company of those who seek him,
>    who seek the face of the *God of Jacob.*

In this reading the pilgrimage is, of course, being made by Israelites, the descendants of Jacob, who now ask to enter the temple. They seek the face of their God. But that is the more streamlined version derived from the Septuagint, the Greek translation of the Bible. The Hebrew text has the more difficult reading: those who come to the temple seek Jacob; that is, they seek the face of the true Israel. They seek the right society as God wills it, in order to find their way through and beyond that society to the true God.

In that case, though, these pilgrims can only be people from among the nations who seek entry into the People of God. Psalm 23 had already traced their dangerous journey and ultimate arrival. Psalm 24 takes up a very particular detail from the scene of their arrival in Jerusalem: their passage through the gates into the temple precinct. It is possible that in the ritual ceremony of admission a priest shouted from without, as soon as a group of pilgrims arrived at the gate:

> Lift up your heads, O gates!
>   and be lifted up, O ancient doors!
>   that the King of glory may come in. (Ps 24:7)

For me these verses are the most stirring in the whole theological fabric of Psalms 22–24, because they say that the King of glory does not wait in the temple for the Gentiles to enter; instead, this King enters into his temple *with them*. So the Holy One was always with them, on the road with them in their long journey from the gods to the true God. What a statement that is for all those in our neo-pagan society who seek the truth but have no idea what that truth ought to look like! And what a promise it is to us, the Gentile Christians, who are still on the way to the dignity of Israel!

One question still remains from our journey through Psalms 22–24: if, in Psalm 23 ("The LORD is my shepherd"), the voice of the one praying represents the nations on pilgrimage to Zion, what about Israel? We already saw that Psalm 23 repeatedly alludes to Israel's history in the wilderness. Are those references no longer valid? Has Israel been excluded from Psalm 23? Certainly not! The psalm continues to speak of Israel *also*; it is just that a second subject has been added.

Theologically this means that the Gentiles who sought a share in the election of Israel cannot be dispensed from Israel's history. They have to follow Israel's path. They too have to dare an Exodus, let themselves be led through the wilderness, and become People of God together with Israel. The original sense of Psalm 23 is thus not destroyed by its being embedded between Psalms 22 and 24; instead, it has acquired a new dimension.

## Our tongues filled with shouts of joy

As we close this chapter we may ask again: what do the Psalms mean for us? In any case they open up tremendous spaces toward the past and the future, spaces of wrath and of peace, of sorrow and of joy, of suffering and of consolation. They contain the whole breadth of human existence.

In doing so they propose a new society, one willed by God. It is a society that is the goal of all historical development, the pinnacle of evolution. It is not yet present. But where the Psalms are spoken there are already signs of it. It is a society in which there is no longer any room for evil, a society of justice and peace.

Many people in Israel prayed the Psalms. Jesus prayed them. The early Christian communities prayed them and drew strength from them. In the young church when catechumens were led to baptism in the Easter Vigil and were allowed to receive the Eucharist for the first time they prayed Psalm 23 beforehand: "The LORD is now [for the future] my shepherd." No book of the Old Testament is quoted so often in the New as is the Psalter. The church considers the Psalms so fundamental that it has made the Psalter its basic prayer book. Our loveliest hymns constantly quote the Psalms—much more often than we imagine.

The language of the Psalms is always young, even though it is old. Whoever prays the Psalms enters into a space in which the whole history of God is gathered together. Those who pray them depart Egypt together with Israel, sit by the canals of Babylon, stand beneath the cross and hear Jesus cry: "My God, my God, why have you forsaken me?" But they also speak together with all those whom God has liberated:

> When the LORD restored the fortunes of Zion,
>     we were like those who dream.
> Then our mouth was filled with laughter,
>     and our tongue with shouts of joy. (Ps 126:1-2)

Those who pray the Psalms are sheltered by God as they travel; indeed, they have already arrived at home.

*Chapter 8*

# Meditation Makes History Present

Do I dare to write a chapter on meditation in this book? I am almost afraid to, because in recent decades whole bushels of books on that subject have appeared on the shelves, offering much that is good and well-ripened but also much that is unripe and wormy. There are probably more books on meditation than there are people who really meditate. In recent decades meditation has not only become one of our big words; it is also big business. Even so, I will dare to include this chapter. Surely it ought to be helpful to point out, again and again, what is distinctively Christian—in this area especially.

## Surrendering the will?

I go into a bookshop and pull a book at random from the well-filled shelves on esotericism. It is called *Wisdom from Silence Within: Meditations on the Inner Light*.[1] I can see very quickly that this little book is thoroughly representative of a broad current of contemporary introductions to meditation. On the cover there is a Buddha with closed eyes in mild, contented repose. He desires nothing.

---

1. Gatha Wandel, *Innere Weisheit aus der Stille: Meditationen zum inneren Licht* (Darmstadt: Schirner, 2007). Translation LMM.

He breathes smilingly into himself. The back cover promises me "easy exercises" with the help of which I can achieve "contact with my inner soul-self," access to the "divine source within me." The introduction to the book tells me that the goal of the exercises is "a state of deep meditation" in which I will "let go of all willing and forget myself." In this "emptiness" there is "nothing"—and at the same time it contains "everything."

But at this point my difficulties are already beginning. How far may the will extend, and where does no-longer-willing begin? The author, Gatha Wandel, *wants* to teach me something and I *want* to learn something, but I am supposed to let go of all willing. Should I want to read her book, or not? That I am supposed to forget myself in the process makes the whole thing even more difficult for me. Must I will to forget myself, or does that self-forgetting creep in, unnoticed, the way sleep comes?

No, according to Gatha Wandel in the second chapter of her book my suffering comes from the fact that I am always "wanting something." This condition of constant wanting is "self-created." That is, I "sowed the seeds" of my present suffering "in this or a former life." But I can work off all this suffering and all my wounds; I can heal myself "with great patience and self-surrender." It may take many years, but it can be done. I must only "believe in myself." I require only "enough courage, surrender, and self-discipline" in order to change my life, because "who else can do it, other than we ourselves?"

Now I am really confused. It seems that I need courage and self-discipline; I must change my life. That much is clear to me. But evidently that requires quite a lot of "willing"—and yet I am not supposed to will anything. How can I escape this dilemma? Maybe the solution is in the next chapters. There I learn that I should apply my "power of thought" to "create beautiful, beneficial, and healing images" within myself.

> For example, we imagine a wondrously beautiful landscape in summer; warm breezes waft the scents of flowers to us. We see a pond before us with turquoise-hued waters; glorious water lilies float there and emit their soft scents. Dragonflies flit about, frogs peep. A soft, warm wind is blowing. There are sweet scents everywhere.

According to Wandel such "visualizations" enable us to approach our "soul-self." Then the soul can "receive cosmic information."

> In this way in times past, for example, the highly developed Pharaonic cultures in Egypt obtained "divine" information and then translated it into the visible world. Information can come in the form of images, lights, sounds, smells, dreams, thoughts, or feelings.

So maybe I don't need to will what is decisive. The "cosmic" or "divine" information will come to me of itself; I only have to prepare my soul through "visualizations." And that happens in meditation.

I will skip over all the preparations, such as the right way to sit, folding the hands and then receptively opening them again, closing my eyes, and so on, and go directly to the essentials the author wants to teach me:

> Breathing in, you receive the fresh energy of the beginnings and cosmic light from the center of the universe. Breathing out, you bring the light into your lower torso.

> . . .

> When your trunk is filled with light and power you will gradually fill your heart and your whole body with cosmic light as well.

> . . .

> Then you prepare yourself to encounter your true self. That soul-essence is already waiting for you. Ask it to show itself to you. You will quickly receive an idea of it.

> . . .

> Your innermost being is perfect; it is full of goodheartedness and wisdom. It is the holy in you, it is what you truly are, from your heavenly origins. That being is always present and never leaves you. It embodies everything you have always sought.

> . . .

But now you are always in contact with the light within you.—
You are that light.

There is a biographical sketch at the end of the book. Here the author's education (evidently accomplished by herself) is described:

Reiki, kinesiology, Pranic healing, crystal healing, trance dancing, family constellation, cranio-sacral therapy, magnified healing, light work, and a great deal more before she met her Qigong teacher and remained with him.

But now let me drop the irony, even though it is really hard not to write satire in the face of so much cosmic light and effective "light work." I will only quote Robert Gernhardt, who in four brief lines said all that needs to be said about the divine inner self evoked by so many esotericists nowadays:

I listen to myself.
There must be something here.
I hear just "peep" and "pip."
I think there's really zip.

Here the critical skeptic Robert Gernhardt is much closer to Christianity than Gatha Wandel, despite her incessant talk of soul, the power of faith, light, confidence, virtue, kindness, love, self-surrender, patience, gentleness, truth, wisdom, and happiness. The song she sings about the soul's light and the treasures of the heart is a mixture of Christianity, Gnosis, watered-down Buddhism, and wellness ideology suited to the market. But primarily she is surrounded by the atmosphere of the wellness industry and its promises. For example, the advertising for a large, popular German spa quotes the expectations of a guest: "I come here because I want to get in contact, finally, with myself. I want to feel good. I want to be completely myself and with myself."

Then, of course, there is the ancient serpent of Gnosis. Gnostic heretics always asserted that human beings in their inmost selves are eternally and by nature divine. They only have to bring out that divine element in themselves through right knowledge (that is, through Gnosis). Valentinus, a Gnostic teacher in the second century CE, wrote in his "Fourth Fragment," as quoted by Clement of Alexandria: "You are *originally immortal*, and children of eternal life" (Clement, *Stromata* 4.13).

Naturally, Gatha Wandel and many other esotericists like her also draw on Christianity. The majority of the concepts she uses (for example, "self-emptying" and "self-forgetfulness") come from Christian mysticism and ascesis. But in her work those concepts have acquired a different background and thus a different meaning.

How could that happen? Is it the author's fault? Or isn't it more the fault of us Christians? We have allowed the great Christian tradition, which assembled an astonishing mass of experience with meditation and inner prayer, to lie fallow and no longer be handed on. When, in previous decades, did pastors even mention such things, much less promote them? We experienced them only in retreats, and even there often in very abstract and rationalized form. In a "normal" parish there was and is no education in prayer and spiritual life. People who have had their own experiences in that field often find no one who can interpret them or help them advance further. Is it any wonder that people who long for spiritual experience draw on very different sources?

As I have said: many of the concepts Gatha Wandel uses are derived from Christian tradition. For example, Christians also know the "inner light of the soul," but with a profound difference: it is not part of our nature but is the light of grace given to us in baptism. And for us, too, there is the "divine" that dwells in us, but that divinity is the Holy Spirit, the soul's guest who has taken up residence in us (Rom 8:9, 11).

## A history of sin

Sacred Scripture, like Robert Gernhardt, takes a very sober view of humanity. The human "innermost self" is anything but perfect, as Gatha Wandel asserts. In the human heart dwell pride, arrogance, envy, greed, hostility—the consequences of a long history of sin in the world. That sinful history became a self-objectifying and deep-rooted context of evil from which no one can escape by his or her own power.

Paul gives a positively existential analysis of how the power of sin sits in unredeemed humanity and works there. It "dwells" in the person, that is, it has reached her or his inmost being. It rules in the mortal body; in Paul's language "flesh" refers to existence itself:

> I do not understand my own actions. For I do not do what I want, but I do the very thing I hate. . . . [I]n fact it is no longer I that do it, but sin that dwells within me. For I know that nothing good dwells within me, that is, in my flesh. I can will what is right, but I cannot do it. For I do not do the good I want, but the evil I do not want is what I do. (Rom 7:15-19)

There is nothing here about a "light-filled, perfect soul-being," nothing about a "true self" that cannot be touched by false images and bad models of behavior. Instead we are to understand that the whole of human existence is subject to the power of sin: constant self-praise, unlimited self-care, disordered and boundless greed. Human beings are *not* masters of themselves as many guides to meditation suggest; they are "slaves to sin," torn this way and that, doing what they hate.

This situation of humanity is not, however, natural; it is the product of history. It is the result of a long process of human development imbued with aggression and rivalry. Paul speaks simply of "sin," but he thinks of that sin as a power that should not exist but has spread throughout the world. This is about much more than the history of individuals, even in supposed "previous existences." It is about the history of cultures, societies, ultimately the whole world.

There are potentials for evil that entrap not only individuals but whole families, even whole nations. We only need to think of the unfreedom and inhumanity that National Socialism brought on a whole nation, and the blindness did not begin with Hitler. The roots of that evil extend deep into history. Does Gatha Wandel really believe she could resist such historic forces by "visualizing" water lilies and the scent of flowers?

## A counter-history

The Bible depicts the history of injustice and conflict that erupts in the world again and again. It does so implacably and with great sobriety. But it also depicts a counter-history beginning with Abraham and culminating in Jesus. It is a story of struggle and liberation—from slavery and oppression, from false gods, from injustice and unjust structures. It is not just about individuals; it is also about a just society that lives in such a way that blessing rests on it and peace streams forth from it.

Here we arrive at another and much more serious difficulty with most books on meditation. They not only suggest that the human being is master of the self but pretend that there is no such thing as a society in which individuals are tangled by a thousand threads.

Again the Bible has a much more realistic view. It knows how easily individuals can succumb to the models presented by society. It knows the extent to which they are exposed to the spirit of the times—to what is ordinary, to what "they" do because others are also doing it, to what is propagated by the opinion makers and manipulators. Hence God confronts the powers of evil not only with individual prophets and saints but with a whole people. God wants to have a people in the world—a people from which blessing can come for the whole world. That is a baseline in Old and New Testament theology.

Of course, all the problems that exist everywhere in society are present in that people also, all over again. Here too are injustice, rivalry, obsession with power, vengefulness, temptation. Evil is here as well. But here are also Abraham, Moses, and the prophets. Here is the Torah: the social order given by God. Here is the admonitory and liberating memory that whitewashes nothing but instead brings it constantly to memory. Here is the temple where Israel confesses its sin again and again and begs forgiveness. Finally, here is Jesus with his parables, his Sermon on the Mount, his absolute nonviolence, and his giving of himself for others even unto death. Will God succeed in creating salvation for the world in and with this people? It all depends on whether and how that success is achieved. That is the truly staggering question of world history.

## Assembling our whole will

Against this background we must ask: what role can meditation play? It must not be focused individualistically, solely on the one person and her or his salvation. It must not be concerned only with the "inner soul-self." It cannot busy itself with turquoise-hued water, whirring dragonflies, and peeping frogs. It most certainly may not "abandon all willing," because when God acts in the world and creates salvation there we must want to have something to do with that divine action. We have to want it and ask for it, long for it and desire it. Then there is nothing more worthy of our actions than seeing God's work and praising God for it. What is needed is not "abandoning all willing" but instead a willing that gathers up one's whole existence.

I consider it a lunatic theory, utterly false to the nature of humanity, to say that one should not "will." Of course, I may will; I cannot do otherwise. I only have to will what is right and in the right way. I should will with my whole heart, my whole soul, all my thoughts, and all my strength what God wills. I must will God's very self, desire it and long for it.

Certainly in doing so I must know that I can only be endowed by God with this right willing, and therefore I await it as a gift; I am drawn to it. I long for it and hope for it as I long and hope for God's very self.

Obviously one who meditates should apply all the bodily and mental techniques that aid in gathering the self together. One may and must, while meditating, flee from the many voices that constantly invade one's consciousness from outside and above all those that arise from within the self. One should fence off one's own thoughts as they constantly try to break through. The spirit should be directed only to the one essential thing. Those who meditate should even let everything happen that helps them to become "empty." But all that must not be for one's own purposes; it is only preparation for the one thing: turning wholly and solely toward God's history in the world.

True meditation cannot be unworldly; it is radically engaged with the world. It most certainly cannot be objectless. Its object is God and God's history with the world.

## Narrative as basic biblical structure

So how do we encounter that history? Only by telling stories! After all, history can only be told, because it is not simply a chaotic heap of mere facts. Are there really such things as "mere facts"? Don't facts always approach us as already interpreted? However that may be, in any case the so-called facts must be organized and related to other facts and to "before" and "after." But that in itself involves interpretation, and nothing does that better than narrative.

Because the subject of the Bible is the history that has taken place between God and the world and between God and God's people, its inner structure is that of narrative. It begins by telling how God created the world. It tells of sin breaking into the world. It narrates the call of Abraham, the history of Isaac and Jacob. It tells of the exodus from Egypt. One of Israel's confessions of faith is:

> A wandering Aramean was my ancestor; he went down into Egypt and lived there as an alien, few in number, and there he became a great nation, mighty and populous. When the Egyptians treated us harshly and afflicted us, by imposing hard labor on us, we cried to the LORD, the God of our ancestors; the LORD heard our voice and saw our affliction, our toil, and our oppression. The LORD brought us out of Egypt with a mighty hand and an outstretched arm, with a terrifying display of power, and with signs and wonders; and he brought us into this place and gave us this land, a land flowing with milk and honey. (Deut 26:5-8)

This central, tightly concentrated text—spoken every year at the offering of first fruits—is a narrative that summarizes an essential part of Israel's history.

Clearly the Bible is not *just* narrative. Scattered throughout it are many other types of texts such as interpretation, instruction, admonition, invocation, consolation, and these types are subdivided into the greatest variety of subgenres, but that does not change the fact that in the Bible all these other text types are built into the narrative. For example, the great law collections in the Old Testament do not stand in isolation but are embedded in narrative.

In the same way, the New Testament letters consist primarily of instruction, admonition, and consolation, but regularly embedded in them are formulas of faith that refer to history, and the letters as a whole stand within a single great narrative. This is so because the New Testament begins with the gospels, continues with the Acts of the Apostles, and ends with the interpretation of history that is the book of Revelation. Recent exegesis has given us this insight, seeing the New Testament for the first time as a single redactional composition and thus as a "unified narrative." Hence it is no surprise that the Christian creed also has a narrative structure:

> . . . born of the Virgin Mary,
> suffered under Pontius Pilate,
> was crucified, died and was buried;
> he descended into hell;
> on the third day he rose again. . . .

In this context it is worth noting that the Qur'an is certainly *not* a narrative. It is altogether instruction and admonition. It does not even have a narrative *frame*. That is connected to the fact that its subject is not, as is the case with the Bible, the history that has taken place between God and the world, or between God and God's people.

This long excursus about *narrative*, the storytelling basic structure of the Bible and all truly Christian texts, was absolutely necessary because it opens up for us the real object of Christian meditation. Its object is not self-emptying; it is most certainly not nothingness, nor is it Nature as such. It is the history of God with the world, more precisely with God's people.

## Complete self-emptying?

I just said that the true object of Christian meditation is not "self-emptying." I did so very deliberately because since Eastern techniques of meditation have come to play a role for Christians also and have acquired the sheen of a new reality we hear more and more talk of "becoming empty." That was made all the easier by the fact that there has long been a similar phenomenon that is simply taken for granted in the Christian spiritual tradition. The ancient teachers of the spiritual life, and above all the Christian mystics, often speak of the soul's freeing itself, letting go, of the night of the senses and the spirit, and so of becoming empty.

But this is just the point at which the difference from genuine (not watered-down Western) Buddhism is clear. The Christian mystic wants to empty the self, become "nothing," but only in order to be completely filled by God and to be fully present for God.

This is how, for example, we should understand the "nothing" in John of the Cross (1542–1591). He does *not* refer to the dissolution of the self but to its being filled with the "all" that is God. Before God the human being is a nothing, but at the same time by turning fully and entirely to God one becomes *wholly oneself*, a person in the fullest sense.

So becoming empty is not the goal but only the precondition for the real thing: the presence of God. In principle we cannot even say it is a precondition that we ourselves have to bring about, because only God can liberate us from the chaos within us and from our enmity toward God. Probably it is, in fact, the turning toward what the Bible tells us about God's acting that really frees us from the self and truly centers us.

The professionals in Buddhism may go on arguing over whether for Siddhartha Gautama this selfless openness—becoming empty of absolutely everything that is—served to free him for something wholly other that no one can name and that is true redemption. I cannot judge that. I only know that for true Buddhists that Other is not God. It has no face. It is not a "thou," not a loving partner. When Buddhists are asked questions pointing in that direction they usually refuse to answer because they regard such questions as false in principle. I also know that Christians who have set themselves wholly on the path to becoming altogether empty have entered into dangerous spaces.

The year 1990 saw the death of the Jesuit priest Hugo Makibi Enomiya-Lassalle, who was known throughout the world for his attempts to integrate Zen methods into Christianity. At first he thought it was not at all about adopting the content of Buddhist teaching but simply about a method leading to mystical prayer. But evidently Father Lassalle then found that the reception of Zen unfolded a logic of its own that led far beyond that initial goal. Toward the end of his life he entered into a painful crisis over his own ideas about faith. One of the diary entries he left behind read:

What if there really is no divine vis-à-vis? . . . A process has begun in me [about which] I [cannot] speak with anyone who remains more or less within "traditional faith." It seems to me that I must not will to stem the process; rather, it is about [entering into] a dark depth where it will steadily become darker, so that maybe one will seek orientation in a straw. A new phase has begun. How long will it last before I reach the other shore? Will I ever experience that?[2]

One should not quote this diary entry without adding that to the end of his life Father Lassalle lived in the most profound fidelity to the church, to Jesus Christ, and to the God of the Bible. Still, he fell into this distress. Was it only the "dark depth" known to all Christian mystics, or was it something more? Was it, perhaps, unavoidable? The objectless meditation of Zen is inseparably linked to the Buddhist worldview and theory of knowledge, and meditation techniques are never mere tools. Whether we will it or not, they convey content. Christians must always ask themselves whether they are compatible with the biblical image of the living God who speaks, who acts, and whose face one may seek.

## Meditation on the natural world?

I have also asserted that the proper object of Christian meditation is not Nature either, in the sense of Gatha Wandel's water lilies and peeping frogs. That too needs explanation because obviously everything in the natural world can be incorporated in meditation, from the ant to the starry heavens. It is only a question of the *way* one approaches Nature.

There is emotionally moving observation of the natural world in the Old Testament, in terms of the possibilities for scientific observation at that time and also with astonished admiration. Take, for example, Psalm 104, where we read:

2. For more on Enomiya-Lassalle see Ursula Baatz, "Hugo M. Enomiya-Lassalle: Zen-Enlightenment and Christianity," in *A Companion to Jesuit Mysticism*, ed. Robert Aleksander Maryks, Brill's Companions to the Christian Tradition (Leiden and Boston: Brill, 2017), 335–57.

You make springs gush forth in the valleys;
 they flow between the hills,
giving drink to every wild animal;
 the wild asses quench their thirst.
By the streams the birds of the air have their habitation;
 they sing among the branches.
From your lofty abode you water the mountains;
 the earth is satisfied with the fruit of your work.
You cause the grass to grow for the cattle,
 and plants for people to use,
to bring forth food from the earth,
 and wine to gladden the human heart,
oil to make the face shine,
 and bread to strengthen the human heart. (Ps 104:10-15)

And so on until the whole visible creation has been listed: wild asses, storks, goats, pikas, young lions—everything is brought into view, but always as God's creation. The "thou" of God is always in the picture:

O LORD, how manifold are your works!
 In wisdom you have made them all;
 the earth is full of your creatures. (Ps 104:24)

We should note that Psalm 104 looks not only to nature; it also considers history. That is to say, nature is embedded in history—human history, inasmuch as humans can besmirch and destroy creation. So at the end of Psalm 104 we read:

Let sinners be consumed from the earth,
 and let the wicked be no more.
Bless the LORD, O my soul.
Praise the LORD! (Ps 104:35)

Since we have schooled our perception to notice the linkage between individual psalms and their context we should take a brief look at the two neighboring psalms between which Psalm 104 has been placed. Psalm 103 is a hymn to God's sovereignty, revealed by God at the Sinai event and pervading all history:

> The LORD works vindication
>> and justice for all who are oppressed.
> He made known his ways to Moses,
>> his acts to the people of Israel.
> The LORD is merciful and gracious,
>> slow to anger and abounding in steadfast love. (Ps 103:6-8)

Likewise, the hymn that follows Psalm 104 is a historical psalm through and through that meditates on the history of the People of God from the ancestors of Israel who traveled through the lands of the earth to the entry into the Promised Land. Thus Psalm 104 is embedded in the memory of God's deeds in history; its praise of creation is bound up in praise of the history that God brings into being.

It is no different for Jesus. He can contemplate the birds of the air that do not sow or reap or gather into barns and yet are fed by God (Matt 6:26). So also the lilies of the field that do not work or spin and yet are more beautifully clad than Solomon (Matt 6:28-29). But that is not some isolated glance at Nature. The subject is the disciples' lack of care; they may give themselves entirely to the preaching of the reign of God without provision for the day to come. Jesus must have viewed the glories of Nature with astonished eyes but without losing sight of the Creator and the reign of God now beginning.

So it remains true that Christian meditation arises out of contemplation of the works of God. That contemplation may include many things: nature, humanity, the world, the whole creation, the Torah, the nature of God. But the frame and underpinning of it all must be God's action in history, for that is the Bible's basic story.

And because God's action reached its high point and goal in Jesus Christ, it is the events in the life of Jesus that must be the primary content of Christian meditation. That was always obvious to the great teachers of the spiritual life; we need only think of the Spiritual Exercises of Ignatius Loyola or the writings of Teresa of Ávila.

## Murmuring the text

But how can this meditation proceed? What path does it take? How does it move forward? The fundamental point here is that we are dealing with a *text*, one we ourselves reproduce.

The text could, of course, be presented to us by someone else; that is, it could be read aloud or told, but that would be more like the situation in the Liturgy of the Word. Meditation has another life-setting (*Sitz im Leben*). In meditating I myself reproduce the text, either by reciting it from memory or by reading it.

We have to be clear about the fact that in the ancient Near East and in antiquity generally, until well into the Christian era, there was a widespread culture of recitation from memory that the majority of people took for granted. Deuteronomy 6:4-7 reads:

> Hear, O Israel: The LORD is our God, the LORD alone. You shall love the LORD your God with all your heart, and with all your soul, and with all your might. Keep these words that I am commanding you today in your heart. Recite them to your children and talk about them when you are at home and when you are away, when you lie down and when you rise.

The book of Deuteronomy speaks here about very concrete events in the lives of Israelites. The text Moses "commands today" is the Torah of Deuteronomy 6–26, hence a very long text. It is to be "written on the hearts of Israel." That means quite simply that everyone in Israel should know it by heart.

How is that supposed to happen? Fathers recited the sections of the text again and again to their children and they repeated them together. In that way they learned the long text by heart, and then they were in a position to recite the text for themselves, that is, to murmur it aloud, in the house and when they were on the road, in the evening before they went to sleep and in the morning when they arose. This was not done primarily to keep from forgetting the text but in order to meditate on it. So within that culture of memory meditating meant speaking the text in a low voice, murmuring it aloud (cp. also Ps 37:30-31).

Jesus must have learned long passages from the Old Testament in just this way and "meditated" on them. He heard the Scriptures recited again and again by his parents, and so he learned them by heart. The early monks meditated on the Psalms in the same way: they murmured them aloud.

It would be good for us, too, to learn some texts of the Bible by heart, to be able to recite basic texts of our faith without a book:

the Our Father, the Glory Be, the Gloria, the Credo, the Confiteor, the Hail Mary. But our present situation is different. We no longer command the mnemonic techniques of the ancient world, nor do we possess the capacious memories of previous generations. Our memory banks are brimful of infinite quantities of information (and misinformation).

But there is one thing we should retain, or recover, from the meditation techniques of the Jews and the early Christians: reading the Bible half aloud, murmuring it. Anyone who has read this far knows that such a practice is already meditation. Meditating is not a science for initiates; it is not a secret teaching that presupposes higher anointing, nor does it require enormous effort. It is something quite simple. For example, it could look something like this:

- I fix a length of time for my meditation, determined altogether by my opportunities and situation.

- To begin with I choose a text that is not too difficult: for example, the gospels or the Acts of the Apostles, 1 Corinthians or Philippians, Genesis or Tobit, Jonah or the Psalter.

- I begin to read, slowly and half aloud, with a pause after every sentence.

- It may be that in the process I will discover that my reading half aloud works like a brake. At first that may be unpleasant. I feel I should read faster; I am used to gliding over the text. It may even be that this way of reading is so unfamiliar to me that I miss a lot. But gradually that will change. The text begins to have an echo. It digs deeper into me. It begins to be alive.

- When a word or a phrase appeals to me I stop there. Maybe I repeat it. I think about what it means for me. I imagine God speaking it to me personally. Then I simply go on reading.

- Even when I don't understand something, I go on reading. Nobody needs to understand everything in a great text. More important than rational comprehension is the tasting of things from within.

- When the fixed time period is over, I stop. The next day I read from the point at which I left off.

- At the end of each session I thank God with a prayer.

## The rosary

Meditation can look something like that. Of course, what I have just described is one particular form of meditation. There are many others—the rosary, for example. What happens when one prays the rosary?

First it is important to know that this meditative prayer also has a number of very different forms: besides the Roman Catholic rosary there are also, for example, the Orthodox and Anglican forms as well as the Christ-rosary of the Lutheran Brotherhood of St. Michael.

The Roman Catholic rosary includes many sequences of Hail Marys, normally fifty repetitions in groups of ten (called "decades"). In each group a clause is inserted that recalls an event from the life of Jesus or his mother Mary. Thus, for example, the Sorrowful Mysteries include five events in Jesus' passion:

The agony in the garden

The scourging at the pillar

The crowning with thorns

The carrying of the cross

The crucifixion

Pope John Paul II introduced a set of Luminous Mysteries that meditate on five earlier events in Jesus' life:

The baptism of Jesus in the Jordan

The wedding feast at Cana

The proclamation of the kingdom

The transfiguration

The institution of the Eucharist

The rhythmically repeated Hail Marys thus form the scaffolding that supports the meditation. Little by little they shape the prayer to the rhythm of breathing, bring peace to the one praying, and create a "space" within which one's gaze can rest on the mystery from the life of Jesus that is central to each decade.

Thus the rosary centers on a series of historical events: God's action for God's people and thus for the world. In that sense the rosary fulfills the already-modest basic condition of Christian meditation: it always has an object. That object is not self-emptying, most certainly not nothingness; it is not Nature as such. It is God's history with the world.

On the other hand, the rosary cannot be about focusing one's whole attention on the meaning of the words one is praying at any one time. That would not only be inhuman but would completely obliterate the function of the constantly repeated Hail Marys, which is to create a "space" within which one comes to a state of quiet so that real meditation can take place. In this way, of course, a certain degree of objectlessness enters into the meditation: the phrases of the Hail Mary that, taken by themselves, have objects of their own become insignificant and a mere "framework." That need not be the case. The real meaning of a Hail Mary can always come through. But in essence the constant repetition of the Hail Mary aims at a deobjectification of the prayer: attention should be drawn more and more toward the mysteries in the life of Jesus.

To go one step further: even the individual "mysteries" that are central to the rosary can be deobjectified. While normally my whole attention is focused on the particular mystery in the life of Jesus proper to each decade—his birth, or his preaching of the reign of God, or his crucifixion—it can happen that even these "objects" fall away, that the spirit may perceive them but in fact is simply before God.

In the midst of the external prayer focusing on the chosen objects of the meditation (namely, the events of our salvation), a sudden peace can come, a deep silence such as only God can give. Seen from without, the prayer continues, but at the same time something has changed. One's heart is altogether surrendered to God, holds fast to God, rests in God and wills only to remain with God.

What I have said about the rosary can happen in every kind of Christian meditation and in every form of Christian prayer. To that extent there is a polar tension in prayer, and most certainly in meditation, that must not be smoothed out and most certainly not dissolved. On the one hand, Christian meditation always has an object: it focuses on God's action in history. But at the same time the texts that speak of that divine action, even while they are being spoken, recede into the background so that the one praying is simply with God, the heart resting in God. There is thus a tension between object orientation and deobjectification.

That tension can also be expressed as a temporal sequence: at certain moments one recites a text, reflects on it, tries to penetrate it—and soon afterward one is simply with God, the texts receding into the background. What is important is only that the objectivity is never altogether lacking. It must remain the basis for everything because the holy God who cannot be grasped in objects or images, who is altogether intangible, has become flesh in Jesus Christ and dwelt among us.

It was necessary at this point to discuss the polarity between "objective" and "objectless" because it shows that there are similarities, and perhaps even commonalities, between the deobjectification in Buddhist and Christian forms of meditation. Certainly profound differences remain: namely, the object orientation in Christian meditation, and in Christian prayer as a whole, that can never be surrendered because it always forms the basis of the prayer. Christian meditation is always about real history, and Christian prayer always deals with the living "thou" of God. The same is true in Judaism.

## Making present

After these clarifications we can turn again to the meditation on texts as such. The texts we are meditating on stem from past centuries; what they relate took place almost two thousand years ago or, if they come from the Old Testament, even earlier. The things they challenge us to or ask of us presuppose a time different from our own. Much that they say appears in a form that is foreign to us. The distance is great—and yet these texts want to speak to us today. Is that possible? The problem is an ancient one. The fifth chapter of the book of Deuteronomy begins this way:

> Moses convened all Israel, and said to them: Hear, O Israel, the statutes and ordinances that I am addressing to you today; you shall learn them and observe them diligently. The LORD our God made a covenant with us at Horeb. Not with our ancestors did the LORD make this covenant, but with us, who are all of us here alive today. The LORD spoke with you face to face at the mountain, out of the fire. (Deut 5:1-4)

According to the structure of the book of Deuteronomy, Moses says this to a generation that had not experienced the exodus from Egypt or the events at the mountain of God, Sinai. The addressees are part of the second generation. The first is already dead. Even so, Moses says it all happened "with us," the progeny. The Lord spoke at that time "to us," we who stand here today. The event at the mountain of God is thus not in the past. It is made present when the text is spoken. In the next chapter we read:

> When your children ask you in time to come, "What is the meaning of the decrees and the statutes and the ordinances that the LORD our God has commanded you?" then you shall say to your children, "We were Pharaoh's slaves in Egypt, but the LORD brought us out of Egypt with a mighty hand. The LORD displayed before our eyes great and awesome signs and wonders against Egypt, against Pharaoh and all his household. He brought us out from there in order to bring us in, to give us the land that he promised on oath to our ancestors. Then the LORD commanded us to observe all these statutes, to fear the LORD our God, for our lasting good, so as to keep us alive, as is now the case. (Deut 6:20-24)

This text too makes it clear that the generation that had no experience of the exodus from Egypt may speak this way and must regard itself as if it had then been present. "The LORD brought *us* out of Egypt." This is not about "as if." It is reality. And this reality is valid, of course, not only for the time when the book of

Deuteronomy was written. It is valid for us also as we read the biblical texts today. How is that possible?

An initial answer must be: because we can be led into situations similar to those in ancient Israel. God leads us, too, out of the unfreedoms of our lives. We too are tested, just as Israel was tested in the wilderness. We also receive God's commandments, meant to give us life.

All that is certainly correct, but it is not enough. The realization, the making-present that appears at important moments in the Bible means much more than that. The letter to the Hebrews shows us that, in what is perhaps its most significant passage, Hebrews 12:18-24. This text also looks back again to the Sinai event but distinguishes Christian worship from it. What once happened for Israel at the mountain of God—according to the theology of Hebrews—was only preliminary, "a shadow of the good things to come" (Heb 10:1), a foretaste of what would become definitive reality through Christ:

> You have not come to something that can be touched, a blazing fire, and darkness, and gloom, and a tempest, and the sound of a trumpet, and a voice whose words made the hearers beg that not another word be spoken to them. . . . But you have come to Mount Zion and to the city of the living God, the heavenly Jerusalem, and to innumerable angels in festal gathering, and to the assembly of the firstborn who are enrolled in heaven, and to God the judge of all, and to the spirits of the righteous made perfect, and to Jesus, the mediator of a new covenant, and to the sprinkled blood that speaks a better word than the blood of Abel. (Heb 12:18-19, 22-24)

It is clear that here the assembly of the New Covenant is compared with the assembly of Israel at Sinai. As Israel approached Sinai, so now the New Testament People of God has approached the true Zion, the heavenly Jerusalem. When did that happen; when does it happen? It happens primarily in public worship: the text speaks of a "festal gathering" and of "the sprinkled blood," that is, Jesus' sacrificial death. But this cultic assembly explodes every space and all time. Here is gathered the church, with Jesus Christ the mediator, with all the angels and all the righteous who have died.

Heaven and earth are joined. In this assembly is completed, in contrastive fashion, what once happened at Sinai: now the people really approach and the blood that has been shed is efficacious.

Following the theology of Hebrews we may therefore say that there is a realization, a making-present, in which the limits of space and time dissolve. The true location of that realization is worship, where a memorial is celebrated that incorporates past history. Here what formerly happened becomes present. This is possible— again according to Hebrews—because there is a heavenly reality in which all history is present and perfected and through which it can be made present to us also. Jesus Christ has entered into this heavenly reality through his resurrection and exaltation; indeed, he constituted it through his resurrection.

Private meditation is certainly not the same thing as Christian public worship, but neither is it the case that it has nothing at all to do with such worship. It prepares us for it. It takes place close to it and within the light it sheds. It tastes, in retrospect, of its fruits.

But what, exactly, is the link between meditation and public worship? That link is history. Christian meditation is concerned with history—the deeds of God in history—and Christian worship centers on the *memoria*, the cultic remembrance of the event that turned and perfected all history: the death and resurrection of Jesus Christ.

So we are now prepared to turn our attention to the climax of all Christian prayer: the Eucharistic Prayer. In it are concentrated the praise, the thanksgiving, and all the petitions of our lives—and, of course, all the meditation in which we recall God's mighty works.

*Chapter 9*

# What Happens in the Eucharistic Prayer?

## Layer upon layer

At some point or other each of us has read a book on archaeology or seen television programs about excavations. I always find such accounts fascinating. What draws me most is how the archaeologists, with endless patience, lift up layer after layer and then, at some point, reach the oldest level of settlement.

This is especially evident when one stands on top of the mountain of rubble from the ancient city of Jericho, the Tell es-Sultan. It is like looking at a Black Forest cake with a piece cut out: a whole variety of layers of settlement, down to the depths of the Tell. It is astonishing to hear that the oldest layer (which remains out of sight) stems from the period around 11,000 BCE.

The comparison has its limits. In a certain sense we could liken the Mass to such a dig: in the course of centuries it has built up layer after layer until it reached the form we are familiar with today. It would be fascinating to sound it, too, as an archaeologist might.

We could, for example, consider the form of the Mass before the great liturgical reform that began with Vatican II—in other words, the so-called Tridentine Mass. Or we could look at the shape of the eucharistic celebration before the Council of Trent, or its form before Charlemagne. Then we would see, among other things, that from the eighth century onward, and the Frankish revision of the Roman liturgy that took place at that time, the Eucharistic Prayer (the "Canon") was prayed *silently* by the priest. From then on, and for a very long time, the Eucharistic Prayer was seen as something secret and mysterious, a holy space that only the priest was allowed to enter. The congregation were supposed to be present in worshipful silence.

Things would get even more interesting if we then pressed further and further back, perhaps to the time of the imperial church, and visited one of the great Roman "station Masses"—for example, in the basilica of St. Paul Outside the Walls or that of St. Peter. And, of course, there is the very important question of how the form of the eucharistic celebration developed in the eastern and southern parts of the empire—in North Africa, in Egypt, in Syria, in Persia, in Byzantium, in Armenia. Obviously we cannot do all that here, even though it would be very exciting. Our subject is the Eucharistic Prayer. Even so, we have to do a little archaeological digging here also as regards the Eucharistic Prayer itself—and that in itself is fascinating.

## What is the "Eucharistic Prayer"?

To begin at the beginning, I have used the phrase "Eucharistic Prayer," and it is clear what that means: the great central section of the Mass that begins with the Preface and ends with the great Doxology before the Our Father. But this part of the Mass was not always called the "Eucharistic Prayer." That phrase is relatively new. It was probably created in the early twentieth century by the Orientalist and liturgist Anton Baumstark (1872–1948). Baumstark's special subject was the eucharistic prayers of the ancient Eastern liturgies, and he applied the term not only to the prayers of the eucharistic celebration but also to the great consecratory prayers of the other sacraments, such as the consecration of a bishop.

If I open my old preconciliar missal I see that it does not use the words "Eucharistic Prayer" at all; instead, it speaks of the "Canon," or more precisely of the "Canon Missae" (Canon of the Mass), and the Preface is clearly distinguished from it by an illustration and even a full-page crucifix. That development came about because the Canon of the Roman Mass always had the same wording, beginning with the *Te igitur*, the first prayer after the *Sanctus*. There was no selection of forms, and hence also the name "Canon." The word "canon" means a rule, a measuring line, a standard. There were many Prefaces for different liturgical seasons and feasts. Hence the sharp division in the old missal between Preface and Canon. That division began in the Gallican liturgies. Regrettably, it brought about the loss of any sense of the unity of the Eucharistic Prayer. Hence the modern term is a clear advance over the older missals with their separation of Preface and Canon. In the East, over the ages, the word has been not "Canon" but *anaphora*, "presentation," referring to the whole Eucharistic Prayer.

## The Mass in the second century

This already tells us something about the most important concept in this chapter. Now we will take a giant step back to the beginning. To continue the metaphor: we are digging down to one of the most ancient accounts of the form of the eucharistic celebration, namely, the one given by the theologian Justin in his *Apology*, written around the year 150 for the Roman emperor, Antoninus Pius. There, in chapter 65, Justin speaks first about the eucharistic celebration that followed baptism:

> But we, after we have thus washed him who has been convinced and has assented to our teaching, bring him to the place where those who are called brethren are assembled, in order that we may offer hearty prayers in common for ourselves and for the baptized [illuminated] person, and for all others in every place. . . . Having ended the prayers, we salute one another with a kiss. There is then brought to the president of the brethren bread and a cup of wine mixed with water; and he, taking them, gives praise and glory to the Father of the universe, through the name of the Son and of the Holy Ghost, and offers thanks at considerable length for our being counted worthy to receive these things at His hands. And when he has concluded the prayers and thanksgivings, all the people present express their assent by saying Amen. This word Amen answers in the

Hebrew language to γένοιτο [so be it]. And when the president has given thanks, and all the people have expressed their assent, those who are called by us deacons give to each of those present to partake of the bread and wine mixed with water over which the thanksgiving was pronounced, and to those who are absent they carry away a portion.

A little later, in chapter 67, Justin describes the Eucharist as it is celebrated apart from the baptismal ceremony. The two accounts are complementary:

And on the day called Sunday, all who live in cities or in the country gather together to one place, and the memoirs of the apostles or the writings of the prophets are read, as long as time permits; then, when the reader has ceased, the president verbally instructs, and exhorts to the imitation of these good things. Then we all rise together and pray, and, as we before said, when our prayer is ended, bread and wine and water are brought, and the president in like manner offers prayers and thanksgivings, according to his ability, and the people assent, saying Amen; and there is a distribution to each, and a participation of that over which thanks have been given, and to those who are absent a portion is sent by the deacons.[1]

In this appeal to the emperor, Justin defends the Christian communities against calumnies. That, of course, forms the framework of his presentation. Even so, his two accounts of the eucharistic celebration are of incalculable value to us because we can derive a great deal about the form of the Mass around the middle of the second century from them. Here are the most important aspects of the two accounts:

1.  The communities gather on Sunday, in Judaism the first day of the week. In Roman terms it is the day devoted to the Sun God. But for Christians it had long since become "the Lord's Day," the day of the Risen One who was regarded as the "Sun of Justice."

---

1. Text available at http://www.newadvent.org/fathers/0126.htm.

2. The Sunday assembly begins with a Liturgy of the Word made up of readings from the Old Testament and from the "memoirs of the apostles" (that is, the gospels). They are read by a "lector," but only "as long as time permits." What does that mean? Quite simply: Sundays, until the year 321, were workdays. It was only under Constantine that Sunday became an official day of rest. Supposing, then, that in the time before Constantine the eucharistic celebration took place in the early morning, the time was limited: the poorer believers had to get to work. In any case, the Roman governor Pliny the Younger, when he interrogated a group of Christians, learned that they regularly gathered *stato die ante lucem,* "on a fixed day . . . before dawn" (Pliny, *Letter to Trajan* 10.96). That could have been the Sunday Eucharist.

3. After these lessons the "president" gives a homily, interpreting the texts that were read.

4. Then all stand and offer prayers; these are clearly what we call the "petitions" or "Prayers of the People." The liturgical reform after Vatican II restored those prayers to us. They had disappeared from the Roman liturgy very early because the Eucharistic Prayer came to contain more and more petitions. The prayers survived only on Good Friday. The fact that they are now a regular part of the liturgy is a return to the church's early times.

5. After the petitions, all exchange the kiss of peace. That sets the seal on the Liturgy of the Word. The kiss of peace represents mutual reconciliation; it is a consequence of the texts that have been read and must precede the eucharistic celebration. It may be that the kiss of peace will soon shift back to its earlier, and appropriate, location within the liturgy.

6. After the kiss of peace bread, wine, and water (for mixing with the wine, as was common in that time) are brought; this corresponds to our Preparation of the Gifts.

7. Then the "president" of the eucharistic celebration, that is, the bishop, speaks "prayers and thanksgivings, according

to his ability." This is precisely what we today call the Eucharistic Prayer. We sense from the way Justin speaks of this "long thanksgiving" that for him this is the center of the eucharistic celebration. It is at this point that his descriptions are most detailed. In particular:

a) He calls the Eucharistic Prayer "praise and glory," "prayers and thanksgivings," or simply "thanksgiving." This last is the decisive word because Justin describes what is given to the believers as communion "the bread and wine . . . over which the thanksgiving was pronounced," and "that over which thanks have been given"—the gifts over which the solemn thanksgiving has been spoken. In the Greek original Justin's word for that thanksgiving is *eucharistia*; in the Latin translation, *gratiarum actio*. But we should not overlook the fact that Justin also calls the Eucharistic Prayer "praise and glory." The Eucharistic Prayer is not only thanksgiving but always also praise. It is imbued with both.

b) The thanksgiving in praise of God is first of all over the gifts of bread and wine. Thus in terms of its basic structure it is a table prayer. The background is probably the Jewish *berakah*, praise of God (also called "benediction") spoken by the head of the household as a table blessing when beginning a meal with praise over the bread, or when concluding a festive meal with a cup of blessing. The ancient Jewish table prayer over the bread was: "Blessed are You, LORD our God, Ruler of the universe, who brings forth bread from the earth" (*b. Berak.* 6.1). The family and guests respond "Amen." The table blessing over the cup at the end of the meal was more extensive, consisting at a later period of four benedictions, the first three of which were as follows:

> (First benediction): Blessed are you, L-rd our G-d, King of the universe, Who, in His goodness, provides sustenance for the entire world with grace, with kindness, and with mercy. He gives food to all flesh, for His kind-

ness is everlasting. Through His great goodness to us continuously we do not lack [food], and may we never lack food, for the sake of His great Name. For He, benevolent G-d, provides nourishment and sustenance for all, does good to all, and prepares food for all His creatures whom He has created, as it is said: You open Your hand and satisfy the desire of every living thing. Blessed are You, L-rd, who provides food for all. Amen.

(Second benediction): We offer thanks to You, L-rd our G-d, for having given as a heritage to our ancestors a precious, good and spacious land; for having brought us out, L-rd our G-d, from the land of Egypt, and redeemed us from the house of bondage; for Your covenant which You have sealed in our flesh [through circumcision]; for Your Torah which You have taught us; for Your statutes which You have made known to us; for the life, favor, and kindness which You have graciously bestowed upon us; and for the food we eat with which You constantly nourish and sustain us every day, at all times, and at every hour. For all this, L-rd our G-d, we give thanks to You and bless You. . . . Blessed are You, L-rd, for the land and for the sustenance. Amen.

(Third benediction): Have mercy, L-rd our G-d, upon Israel your people, upon Jerusalem Your city, upon Zion the abode of Your glory, upon the kingship of the house of David Your anointed, and upon the great and holy House [= Israel] over which Your Name was proclaimed. Our G-d, our Father, tend us, nourish us, sustain us, feed us, and provide us with plenty; and speedily, L-rd our G-d, grant us relief from all our afflictions. . . . And rebuild Jerusalem the holy city speedily in our days. Blessed are You, L-rd, Who in His mercy rebuilds Jerusalem. Amen.[2]

2. https://www.chabad.org/library/article_cdo/aid/135366/jewish/Birkat-Hamazon-in-English.htm.

I have deliberately quoted this table prayer as an example of Jewish benedictions so we can clearly see the most probable roots of the Eucharistic Prayer at Mass. There is a great deal in favor of the idea that it originated in the Jewish *berakah*, or the sequence of the *berakoth* that frames a festal meal.

What is important here is that the Jewish *berakah* is not only thanksgiving for the bread, the wine, or even the whole meal. It shifts to a thanksgiving for the gifts God has given to God's people Israel throughout its history, especially the gifts of the exodus, the covenant, the Torah, the Land. The *berakoth* we have quoted show all that—and something else: the praise/thanksgiving can be transformed into a petition for the people Israel. We will see that the Eucharistic Prayer also, the great Christian prayer of praise, encompasses all of salvation history—and it too can turn into petition.

Justin speaks only about the *event* of the Eucharistic Prayer; he offers no content. But we can already sense what all this prayer of praise might contain because it comes from Judaism. Here too the central content would be God's saving deeds— above all, God's action through Jesus Christ. Instead of the Land and the holy city Jerusalem, the church's prayer will speak of the "holy church."

c) Because this praise derives from Judaism it is quite naturally addressed to God the Father. Justin says explicitly that God, "the Father of the universe," is the addressee of the Eucharistic Prayer. But another essential element is added, differently from Judaism: the thanksgiving takes place "through the name of the Son and of the Holy Ghost." We will see below in more detail how essential this basic structure is for the Eucharistic Prayer.

d) It is true that the president alone speaks the *eucharistia*, but it is spoken in the name of the assembled community. The presider is its speaker before God. Therefore Justin places great value in the solemn "Amen" of the whole assembly. It is really astonishing that he mentions this apparently insignificant detail at all, but evidently it was important to him. The whole people present must "agree" and "join in."

e) Finally: the president freely formulates the Eucharistic Prayer. It is evident that this was really the case because of the side remark: "the president . . . offers prayers and thanksgivings, according to his ability." A later text from the *Apostolic Tradition* shows what that means:

> It is not at all necessary for him [the bishop] to repeat these same words that we said before, as if recited by rote giving thanks to God, but according to each one's ability he shall pray. If, on the one hand, he has ability to pray sufficiently with a prayer that is honorable, then it is good. But if, on the other hand, he prays and recites a prayer briefly, let no one hinder him, only let him pray being sound in orthodoxy. (*Traditio apostolica* 9.4-5)[3]

So much for what Justin says about the Eucharistic Prayer. In relation to the brevity of his text it is quite a lot. But let us pursue his text on Christian worship to its end.

8. After the Eucharistic Prayer has been recited, the bread and wine of the Eucharist are distributed by the deacons to all those present. The deacons are also responsible for bringing the Eucharist to the homes of those absent: for example, the old and the sick. Incidentally we also learn—though I have not quoted the text at this point—that much more food was distributed than was necessary for the Eucharist. The bishop had to see to it that this part of the gifts was distributed to the poor of the community.

This, then, is what the Christian philosopher and teacher Justin wrote about the eucharistic celebration in his *apologia* for the Christian faith around the year 150. Justin died a martyr in Rome. We are grateful to him still today for his witness to the faith—and

---

3. Paul F. Bradshaw, Maxwell E. Johnson, and L. Edward Phillips, *The Apostolic Tradition: A Commentary*. Hermeneia (Minneapolis: Fortress Press, 2002), 68.

also because he was the first to give us a clear and exact account of the course of the Mass.

## A Eucharistic Prayer in Ephesians?

Probably readers have long since thought: "Fine, that gives us information about the course of the worship service. But at some point a real Eucharistic Prayer must have been written down. Where is the oldest complete surviving Eucharistic Prayer?"

The answer is not so simple. For example, at the beginning of the letter to the Ephesians there is a text praising God and the divine plan of salvation that is formulated altogether in the style of a eucharistic prayer. It begins like a Jewish *berakah* and continues by listing God's saving deeds in a series of participial constructions and relative clauses. I will simply quote the beginning of this *berakah*. In doing so I will not organize the individual elements of the sentence into a sequentially constructed form; I will join them with dashes to make it clear that this is a single sentence, and its construction has something provisional about it:

> Blessed be the God and Father of our Lord Jesus Christ—who has blessed us in Christ with every spiritual blessing in the heavenly places—just as he chose us in Christ before the foundation of the world—to be holy and blameless before him in love—[now that he has] destined us for adoption as his children through Jesus Christ—according to the good pleasure of his will—to the praise of his glorious grace—that he freely bestowed on us in the Beloved—in [whom] we have redemption through his blood—the forgiveness of our trespasses—according to the riches of his grace—that he lavished on us—with all wisdom and insight—[for] he has made known to us the mystery of his will—according to his good pleasure—that he set forth in Christ, as a plan for the fullness of time—to gather up all things in him—things in heaven and things on earth. (Eph 1:3-10)

We sense the peculiarity of this style right away. It is altogether the manner in which a presider at the Eucharist might have begun a eucharistic prayer: this is how people spoke in Late Antiquity when they wanted their speech to be solemn and sacral. The philologist Eduard Norden (1868–1941) investigated this style in his book *Agnostos theos*.[4]

That was also how people spoke when they were formulating freely on the basis of traditional statements. I suspect that the author of Ephesians, someone from the Pauline school, formulated the beginning of the letter in much the same way as was the custom in composing the Eucharistic Prayer at worship. There is no way to prove that, and so we must leave open the question whether Ephesians 1:3-12 represents a fragment or a model of a very ancient Eucharistic Prayer. One thing Ephesians 1:3-12 proves, at all events, is that even in the first century there could have been very solemn prayers of thanksgiving within the liturgy, according to the model of the Jewish *berakah*.

## The table prayer in the *Didachē*

It is very different with the table prayers in the *Didaechē*, which—as we saw—was composed at the beginning of the second century. The *Didachē* is the oldest church order, giving instructions for community life. Above all, it gives orders for baptism and Eucharist. In chapter 9.1-5 we read:

> [Now] concerning the eucharist, thus give thanks [eucharistize]. First, concerning the cup: We give you thanks, our Father, for the holy vine of your servant David which you revealed to us through your servant Jesus. To You [is] the glory forever.
>
> And concerning the broken [loaf]: We give you thanks, our Father, for the life and knowledge which you revealed to us through your servant Jesus. To you [is] the glory forever.
>
> Just as this broken [loaf] was scattered over the hills [as grain], and, having been gathered together, became one; in like fashion, may your church be gathered together from the ends of the earth

---

4. Eduard Norden, *Agnostos theos. Untersuchungen zur Formengeschichte religiöser Rede* (Leipzig and Berlin: Teubner, 1913).

into your kingdom. Because yours is the glory and the power through Jesus Christ forever.

[And] let no one eat or drink from your eucharist except those baptized in the name of [the] Lord, for the Lord has likewise said concerning this: "Do not give what is holy to the dogs."[5]

What I have quoted here is part of an agenda with instructions for the Eucharist, with the words of a *berakah* over the cup and another *berakah* over the bread. It is true that these texts from the *Didachē* are highly disputed. In the first place: why is the sequence cup/bread and not the reverse? Second: why are there no "words of institution"? Many experts propose that the texts quoted refer to a full meal of the community and not to the eucharistic celebration itself.

But it could also be that they do indeed refer to the eucharistic celebration and function as a eucharistic prayer. In that case the quotation of Jesus' words at the Last Supper would be missing. That is not a problem in itself because there are early eucharistic prayers attested from eastern Syria that lack "words of institution." In my opinion the warning at the end, "let no one eat or drink," speaks definitely in favor of the idea that the quoted text functioned as a eucharistic prayer. But however we assess the thanksgivings in the *Didachē*, in any case we have here a model of Christian *berakoth* over bread and wine.

## One of the loveliest Eucharistic Prayers

One of the oldest Eucharistic Prayers we can be sure is genuine is the one from the *Apostolic Tradition* (*Traditio Apostolica*). This prayer has been known for a long time, and in the twentieth century it was attributed, together with the whole *Apostolic Tradition*, to Hippolytus, but more recently some scholars have denied the attribution. For the sake of brevity I will speak, nevertheless, of

---

5. *The Didachē*, chap. 9. From Aaron Milavec, *The Didache: Text, Translation, Analysis, and Commentary* (Collegeville, MN: Liturgical Press, 2003), 23.

"Hippolytus's Eucharistic Prayer." Hippolytus was a highly educated presbyter who worked in Rome at the beginning of the third century. For a time he was an anti-pope, but he died a martyr, reconciled with the church, in the year 235.

The so-called *Apostolic Tradition* is an ancient church order that was repeatedly expanded and lengthened. It is of extraordinary importance for the history of the liturgy. Regrettably, the Greek original has not survived; all we have are Coptic, Arabic, and Ethiopic translations, plus a Latin fragment. The first part of that church order treats of the consecration of a bishop and the subsequent celebration of the Eucharist. In that context it presents a model formula for a eucharistic prayer, intended as a suggestion.

> When he has been made bishop, let all offer the mouth of peace, greeting him because he has been made worthy. And let the deacons offer to him the oblations, and let him, laying [his] hands on it with all the presbytery, say, giving thanks:
>
> > "The Lord [be] with you."
> > And let them all say:
> > "And with your spirit."
> > "Up [with your] hearts."
> > "We have [them] to the Lord."
> > "Let us give thanks to the Lord."
> > "It is worthy and just."
> > And so let him then continue:
> > "We render thanks to you, God,
> > through your beloved Child Jesus Christ,
> > whom in the last times you sent to us
> > as savior and redeemer and angel of your will,
> > who is your inseparable word,
> > through whom you made all things
> > and it was well pleasing to you,
> > you sent from heaven into the virgin's womb,
> > and who conceived in the womb was incarnate
> > and manifested as your Son,
> > born from the Holy Spirit and the virgin;
> > who fulfilling your will
> > and gaining for you a holy people
> > stretched out [his] hands when he was suffering,

that he might release from suffering
those who believed in you;
who when he was being handed over to voluntary suffering,
that he might destroy death
and break the bonds of the devil,
and tread down hell
and illuminate the righteous,
and fix a limit
and manifest the resurrection,
taking bread
[and] giving thanks to you, he said:
'Take, eat, this is my body that will be broken for you.'
Likewise also the cup, saying:
'This is my blood that is shed for you.
When you do this, you do my remembrance.'
Remembering therefore his death and resurrection,
we offer to you the bread and cup,
giving thanks to you because you have held us worthy
to stand before you and minister to you.
And we ask that you would send your Holy Spirit
in the oblation of [your] holy church,
[that] gathering [them] into one
you will give to all who partake of the holy things
[to partake] in the fullness of the Holy Spirit,
for the strengthening of faith in truth,
that we may praise and glorify you
through your Child Jesus Christ,
through whom [be] glory and honor to you,
Father and Son
with the Holy Spirit,
in your holy church,
both now and to the ages of ages.
Amen."[6]

The stylistic similarity to the praise at the beginning of the letter to the Ephesians is obvious. In the first part one relative clause follows another; in the second part the frequent links are accomplished by the use of participles. Translations have to resolve the

6. Bradshaw et al., *Apostolic Tradition*, 4.1-13, at pp. 38, 40.

participles. On the one hand, the result is a deliberately solemn and almost hieratic style. On the other hand, it is typical of freely formulated liturgical speech. The whole Eucharistic Prayer reveals the highest degree of coherence. It flows like one long sentence, and yet it is clearly structured.

It begins with a dialogue between the bishop and the congregation as they mutually acknowledge their community with Christ. The bishop charges the congregation to turn its whole existence toward God. Then the theme of the Eucharistic Prayer—thanksgiving—is introduced.

The second part of the prayer takes up the theme just introduced—*Gratias tibi referimus, deus* (We give thanks to you, O God)—and yet this expression of thanks does not happen just anyhow and for any reason. It has a basis. It is a response to God's actions in the world and in history. God's saving deeds in Christ are listed individually, just as in the Creed: his incarnation, his passion, his death on the cross, his descent into the underworld, his resurrection from the dead. But the series begins and is summarized in anticipation by the designation of Christ as Savior, Redeemer, and Messenger of the divine plan of salvation. He is the Logos of God through whom all things were made.

The thanksgiving for God's saving deeds is followed, without interruption, by an "account of institution" in the same relative-clause style. The Last Supper is thus a saving deed of God like those listed before—and therefore it is seamlessly incorporated into the thanksgiving for what God has done through Christ. The words of "institution" are therefore themselves thanksgiving, and consequently bread and wine could be called "the things over which thanks have been given" in the early church, as we saw with Justin.

The fourth part of the Eucharistic Prayer makes a new beginning. *Memores igitur*: "Therefore, remembering." What comes next is no longer thanksgiving but the solemn offering of bread and wine in memory of what Christ commanded at his last meal. The Latin here is *offerimus*, which is a *terminus technicus* of sacrificial language. However, the presentation then immediately becomes thanksgiving again: "giving thanks to You" that we are permitted to stand here and celebrate this memorial.

The fifth part of the Eucharistic Prayer is, for the first time, "petition." We have seen, in fact, that the *berakah*, the Jewish praise of God, can turn to petition, and that happens here as well. At this point the Eucharistic Prayer asks God the Father to send the Holy Spirit upon the bread and wine, thus fulfilling the gifts that were brought before God in the previous "offering." Evidently this means that the Spirit is asked to make them pleasing to God and transform them—though that is more assumed than said. What *is* said explicitly is that the Holy Spirit, transforming the gifts, is likewise asked to fill and transform the assembled believers so that they may be of one mind and be strengthened in faith and truth. Liturgists call this petition for the Holy Spirit, which has become more and more important and is now essential to every Eucharistic Prayer, the "epiclesis"—the summoning or "calling down." What is surprising in Hippolytus's Eucharistic Prayer is that the summoning of the Holy Spirit on the believers, and their transformation, occupies much more space than the request regarding the bread and wine.

Very skillfully and almost without transition the Eucharistic Prayer draws us again to praise in its sixth section, so that the prayer *as a whole* is praise and thanksgiving. The thanksgiving now takes the form of the solemn doxology offered to the Father through the Son and the Holy Spirit in the church. Thereby—as we saw in the first chapter—the basic structure of all Christian prayer is uttered. It is directed *to* the Father *through* the Son *in* the Holy Spirit, that is, in the church. But that prayer structure applies not only to the Eucharistic Prayer. It belongs to all liturgical prayer. Through Christ in the Holy Spirit to the Father—that is the great prayer movement of the liturgy, and it should also be the basic movement of our personal prayer. It is already present in the Our Father.

The seventh part of the Eucharistic Prayer is the assenting and affirming "Amen" of the community. The bishop has given thanks in their name; now the assembly affirms everything spoken by the bishop. It ratifies the Eucharistic Prayer not only in words but by its very existence. In this way the whole Eucharistic Prayer is framed by the words of the assembly, at the beginning and at the end.

## Accretions and changes

I have deliberately given a detailed description of the *form* of the Eucharistic Prayer attributed to Hippolytus because in essentials it is *still today* the form of our Eucharistic Prayer. But we can perceive today's basic structure more sharply and clearly in Hippolytus because in the meantime, in comparison with it, the Eucharistic Prayer has experienced expansions and thus also changes in its structure. Let me list some of the changes:

1. One of the most important changes was the insertion of the *Sanctus*, by means of which the remembrance of God's saving deeds became a separate prayer of thanksgiving, the so-called Preface. With some exceptions (for example, in Eucharistic Prayer IV) the deeds of God are now recited *before the Sanctus*. We can see that very clearly in Eucharistic Prayer II: what in Hippolytus was the memorial ("anamnetic") part of the prayer is now almost completely absorbed in the Preface. But something else results from the insertion of the *Sanctus*: the dialogic structure of the Eucharistic Prayer is strengthened, since the "Holy, Holy, Holy" is spoken or sung by the *assembly*.

2. We do not know precisely when the "Holy, Holy, Holy" entered the Mass liturgy. Jewish prayers already contained the "Holy, Holy, Holy." In any case the insertion of the *Sanctus* was a highly significant expansion of the Eucharistic Prayer since, after all, the first part of the *Sanctus* refers to a heavenly liturgy as described by Isaiah in his call vision. Seraphim surround God's throne and call to one another: "Holy, holy, holy is the LORD of hosts; the whole earth is full of his glory" (Isa 6:3). There is the greatest theological weight in the fact that now the earthly assembly may utter the "Holy, Holy, Holy" of the angels. In doing so they become participants in the heavenly liturgy. When they assemble and praise God in the Eucharistic Prayer, giving thanks, then heaven and earth are joined. The assembly has already entered into the heavenly sphere, "to innumerable angels in festal gathering," as Hebrews says (12:22-24). It is already a participant in the eternal praise of

God. The *Sanctus* thus shows that the church's liturgy is and always has been a participation in the heavenly liturgy.

3. Later eucharistic prayers were also expanded by numerous petitions. Within the one great thanksgiving there are prayers for the whole church, for the pope, for the bishop, for the dead, sometimes for the newly baptized or those estranged from the faith. In the Gallican liturgy even the names of donors were listed—the closer to the "account of institution" the better. Do such petitions disrupt the form of the thanksgiving, or even shatter it?

   By no means! We have already seen that the shift between praise and thanksgiving is altogether characteristic of the Jewish *berakah*. But above all: the petitions within the Eucharistic Prayer have a *gathering* function. They are intended to bring everyone together in the fundamental action of the church, the Eucharistic Prayer—those near and far, the living and the dead, the familiar and unknown saints—so that the whole church may be present when this great prayer of praise is brought before God. Hence the pope must also be named and, together with the local bishop, at least abstractly "all bishops" and, in Eucharistic Prayer III, "the entire people you have gained for you own."

4. Today's Eucharistic Prayer I, that is, the Roman Canon, which—at least in its basic form—dominated in the West from the fourth century onward, contains a broadly structured theology of sacrifice that shapes nearly every section of this classic Eucharistic Prayer:

   > accept . . . these holy and unblemished sacrifices, which we offer you . . .[7]

   > For them we offer this sacrifice of praise, and they themselves dedicate it to you . . .[8]

---

7. *The Roman Missal*: accept . . . these gifts, these offerings, these holy and unblemished sacrifices, which we offer you . . .

8. *The Roman Missal*: For them, we offer you this sacrifice of praise or they offer it for themselves and all who are dear to them . . .

Graciously accept, O God, these gifts of your servants . . .[9]

O God, give the fullness of blessing to these gifts and accept them as your own. Make them for us, in the Spirit, a true sacrifice that is pleasing to you . . .[10]

So from the gifts you have given us we bring you, the Most High God, the pure, holy, and spotless sacrifice: the bread of life and the cup of eternal salvation.[11]

Reconciled and gracious, look upon them and accept them . . .[12]

May your holy angel bear these sacrifices to your heavenly altar, before your divine majesty . . .[13]

This seems almost to shatter the original form of the Eucharistic Prayer. As we have seen, the prayer in its fundamental form is *eucharistia*, thanksgiving and praise, but the first Roman Canon seems to be nothing more than a succession of petitions for blessing and acceptance. However, that is only a first impression because, like Hippolytus's Eucharistic Prayer, it is framed by "Let us give thanks to the Lord, our God" and the concluding doxology. Moreover, at its center, immediately after the so-called "words of institution," we find:

Therefore, gracious Father, we, your servants and your holy people, celebrate the memorial of your Son, our Lord Jesus Christ. We proclaim his lifegiving Passion, his Res-

9. *The Roman Missal*: graciously accept this oblation of our service . . .

10. *The Roman Missal*: Be pleased, O God, we pray, to bless, acknowledge, and approve this offering in every respect; make it spiritual and acceptable . . .

11. *The Roman Missal*: we, your servants and your holy people, offer to your glorious majesty from the gifts that you have given us, this pure victim, this holy victim, this spotless victim, the holy Bread of eternal life and the Chalice of everlasting salvation.

12. *The Roman Missal*: Be pleased to look upon these offerings with a serene and kindly countenance, and to accept them . . .

13. *The Roman Missal*: . . . command that these gifts be borne by the hands of your holy Angel to your altar on high in the sight of your divine majesty . . .

urrection from the dead and his glorious Ascension into heaven . . .[14]

Likewise, within the complex of the various petitions that the gifts be accepted, the prayer maintains that this is about remembering God's great deeds culminating in God's saving action in Jesus Christ. Moreover, a theology of sacrifice had a place even in Hippolytus's prayer, at a central point after the "words of institution":

> Therefore, remembering his death and resurrection, we offer to you the bread and the chalice . . . And we pray that you would send your Holy Spirit to the oblation of your Holy Church . . . .[15]

So we should not set thanksgiving and prayers of offering in contest with one another. The church thanks God the Father for what has been done in Christ, but that action of the Father was at the same time the action of Jesus—and the action of Jesus was nothing but self-dedication, an existence exclusively "for the many." That is precisely what is meant by sacrifice. We thank God for what God has done in and for us—but what God has done for us was the miracle that there was this One whose life was nothing other than pure devotion.

5. We have seen that the Eucharistic Prayer has a dialogic structure. The Preface begins with a dialogue between the presider and the assembly, and at the end the community affirms the Eucharistic Prayer with its "Amen." The "Holy, Holy, Holy" intensifies the dialogic character of the Eucharistic Prayer. With the reform of the liturgy the role of the community was also strengthened by the addition of an acclamation after the "words of institution" such as: "We proclaim your Death, O

---

14. *The Roman Missal*: Therefore, O Lord, as we celebrate the memorial of the blessed Passion, the Resurrection from the dead, and the glorious Ascension into heaven of Christ, your Son, our Lord, we, your servants and your holy people . . .

15. *The Roman Missal*.

Lord, and praise[16] your Resurrection until you come again."
This not only strengthens the dialogical structure of the Eucharistic Prayer; "until you come again [in glory]" also places the prayer within an eschatological horizon. In the early church the eschatological orientation of the whole eucharistic celebration dominated. According to the testimony of the *Didachē*, Syrian communities prayed after communion: "Let grace come, and let this world pass away. . . . *Maran atha* [our Lord, come!]." Hippolytus's Eucharistic Prayer likewise reveals this eschatological consciousness: it speaks of the "end of time" when Jesus has come as savior and liberator. This eschatological quality of the prayer has been lost in the Roman Canon. I can find nothing there that might point to it. We can be grateful that this "until you come again" has restored at least a whisper of the eschatological expectation of the early communities.

## Beyond anything magical

The title of this chapter is "What Happens in the Eucharistic Prayer?" We have traveled a long way to get to the point at which we can give an answer to that question. I will try to do so now in the form of theses that will summarize what has already been worked out but at the same time pushes it a little further.

1. The Eucharistic Prayer is a separate unit, from its opening dialogue to the "Amen" that seals it. It has clear contours that make it stand out from the prior preparation of the gifts and the "Our Father" that follows.

2. The Eucharistic Prayer is the church's basic event. We can see this from the fact that for this event the community gathers everyone around it: those near and far, the living and the dead, the clergy and the whole people. The prayers for all of them are not merely petitions; they also function to create community with them.

16. *The Roman Missal*: profess.

3. The Eucharistic Prayer is spoken by the bishop (or a priest, as the bishop's representative) because the whole church must be represented in this prayer, and representation is a basic function of church office. But it is the prayer of the whole assembly. The incorporation of the assembly is shown first by the opening dialogue, then by the insertion of the *Sanctus* recited by all, further by the acclamation of the assembly after the words of institution, and finally by the affirming "Amen" from the whole assembly at the end of the Eucharistic Prayer.

4. The Eucharistic Prayer is a complete unit above all because the whole thing is thanksgiving: to the Father through the Son in the Holy Spirit. This basic thanksgiving structure is ensured by the opening "Let us give thanks to the Lord our God" and the solemn doxology at the end. Inserted prayers for blessing and acceptance do not alter the basic character of the prayer as thanksgiving, nor does the "account of institution," and most certainly not the epiclesis, the summoning of the Holy Spirit. All these elements are integrated into the overall movement of the great thanksgiving.

5. The church's thanksgiving does not float in the ether; it has a grounding: God's saving deeds. That is why they are listed in the Eucharistic Prayer. That listing never aims at completeness. It is found especially in the Preface but it is taken up again in the *anamnesis*, the "remembering" after the "account of institution." *Memores igitur*—"therefore, remembering."

6. God's eschatological saving acts in history are the death and resurrection of Jesus Christ. For these, above all things, the church gives thanks in the Eucharistic Prayer. Therefore in the *anamnesis* after the "account of institution" the death and resurrection of Jesus are always named, without exception. His descent to the ancestors, his ascension, and his return may also be mentioned.

7. From the beginning the church has understood that Jesus' death was by no means accidental or a meaningless tragedy. His death was, for the church, the final summation of his lifelong dedication "for" Israel and the world. Jesus himself anticipated and interpreted the surrender of his life unto

death at his last meal. Therefore it was profoundly meaning-ful to place the memorial of the Last Supper at the center of the Eucharistic Prayer and to thank God for that event, that is, for Jesus' surrender of his life.

8. We cannot emphasize enough that the "account of institu-tion" is itself thanksgiving, simply from the fact that it is embedded in the whole Eucharistic Prayer, but that would be only a formal observation. The "account of institution" is thanksgiving above all because it interprets the death of Jesus as a saving event: "given up for you," "poured out for the many," as the prayer says. Therefore it has the central place within the listing of God's saving deeds in the Eucha-ristic Prayer.

9. This pulls the rug out from under every kind of sacramen-tal magic. The so-called "words of institution" are located within a story, a report, and that report functions not simply as reportage but as thanksgiving to God for Jesus' sacrifice of his life. Christians have only fallen victim to the danger of "transubstantiation magic" when they could not see the in-corporation of the words of institution into the overall frame of the Eucharistic Prayer. The fact that the Eucharistic Prayer was eliminated in some of the churches of the Reformation, so that only the "words of institution" were spoken over the gifts, was the result of a profound misunderstanding. On the Roman Catholic side a comparable misunderstanding was reflected in the fact that some believers visited several churches, one after another, to be present at the consecration and look at the elevated host in each church.

10. The temptation to indulge in sacramental magic is likewise undermined by the fact that our present Eucharistic Prayers include the epiclesis, the summoning of the Holy Spirit. Today—in contrast to Hippolytus's Eucharistic Prayer—it has its place *before* the "account of institution." This sum-moning makes it clear that the transformation of the gifts is not a magic event brought about by the correct utterance of the right formula. Rather, it is pure grace. The Holy Spirit must be implored here also.

11. Another barrier to our being seduced into sacramental magic is placed within the Eucharistic Prayer in that we pray there not only for the transformation of the gifts of bread and wine but at the same time and with the same intensity for the transformation of the assembled community into the body of Christ. That is: the epiclesis begs the Holy Spirit to descend not only on the gifts but also on the gathering. Liturgists speak of a "transformation and communion epiclesis." Hippolytus combines both in a single prayer, which is theologically quite noteworthy. Today's liturgy unfortunately divides them from one another by the so-called "words of institution."

12. Again, the Jewish background of the Eucharistic Prayer makes any kind of sacramental magic impossible. Ultimately the Eucharistic Prayer derives from the Jewish *berakah*, in particular from the extended *berakoth* over the cup of blessing. We have seen that it is just at this point in the Jewish meal that God's saving deeds are memorialized. This "memorial" is, of course, more than merely remembering. It is a making present of the past history of salvation, following the model of Deuteronomy 5:2-3: "The LORD our God made a covenant with us at Horeb. Not with our ancestors did the LORD make this covenant, but with us, who are all of us here alive today." The past is transformed into the present. The church has entered into this basic Jewish understanding of *memoria*, which achieves its ultimate concretion in the becoming-present of Jesus Christ in the eucharistic gifts.

In Jesus the Logos of God has truly become flesh. That incarnation continues in the sacrament of the Eucharist. But it may not be isolated and located solely in the so-called words of institution. The becoming-present of the exalted Lord takes place in the whole event of the Eucharistic Prayer. To put it another way: the whole Eucharistic Prayer is a transformational text. Christ is present in the *memoria* of the church's great prayer of praise.

## Chapter 10

# *Each of Us Has a Personal History of Prayer*

*Theological theories are important, and the church's tradition is still more important. Most important of all is Sacred Scripture, the word of the living God and likewise the oldest faith-tradition of the church. But all that must always be bound up with experiences of faith that are personal to every individual Christian. Especially with regard to prayer, each of us has her or his own history. This last chapter in my book attempts to sketch the prayer history of a single individual, representative for many other stories that may have been very similar or may, instead, have followed an altogether different course.*

His mother must have taught him his first prayers when he was very young: morning and evening prayer, table prayers, and one to his guardian angel. He can no longer remember the details. He is not even sure whether his mother sat on his bed in the evening, told him a story, and prayed with him. But he can still remember his childhood prayers, word for word.

He still uses some of them today: not because their language or their theology was especially good but because they have a place deep in his soul. One of them did not rhyme and was the best of them all. It was:

> The eyes of all wait upon you, O Lord,
> and you give them their food in due season.
> You open wide your hand
> and fill every living creature with your blessing.[1]

It was many years before he noticed that the prayer comes from Psalm 145. Today he asks himself why we do not teach our children more psalms or psalm verses. They would be much better than most "children's prayers."

❧

But there is one prayer that does rhyme, that sounds like a child's prayer, and yet is couched in high-quality language. It is the well-known "Evening Song" [Abendlied] by Luise Hensel (1798–1876):

> Weary am I and go to rest,
> Closing both my eyes—
> Father! let your eyes instead
> Look down where I lie!
>
> If today I have done wrong,
> dear God, please look away!
> Your great grace and Jesus' blood
> restore whatever's gone astray.
>
> All those who are near to me,
> O God! keep in your hand.
> Every person, big and small,
> lives within your care.
>
> To every weary heart send rest,
> close every tearful eye.
> Let the moon stand there on high
> and watch the silent world.[2]

---

1. From Ps 145:15-16. Translation (adapted) from *The Book of Common Prayer* (1979).
2. Translation LMM.

Everything is in harmony here: the images, the rhyme, the rhythm. It has the simple perspective of a child, but behind its simplicity stands a woman whose innermost self was like a volcano. Without faith, she said, she would have gone crazy, would have committed suicide. This prayer also offers fathers and mothers opportunities to follow a number of threads further. For example, they can ask: "Who are all the people close to you?" Then, when the child begins to list them, they can expand the list. There is another, deeper kind of relationship: the brothers and sisters God has given us in the church. Perhaps they can even explain to their child what "Jesus' blood" means: his "living-entirely-for-others," even to the surrender of his life.

He regrets deeply to this day that when he was a child he did not fall asleep every evening with this beautiful prayer.

On the other hand, he is annoyed that as a child he was introduced to some prayers and songs whose language was unbearably sappy. In preparing for First Communion every child in his group was supposed to keep a notebook to write things down and draw pictures. For the first page of that notebook the pastor dictated the following text, taken from a hymn that was often sung at that time:

Christ, my King, to you alone
swear I my love, all lily-pure,
faithful unto death.

It is wrong to impose such texts on children. They lead them into religious lies because they force the child to promise something it cannot understand at all. The child must almost necessarily get the impression that it is normal to pray in big, empty words. Incidentally, according to German civil law one is only capable of making an oath on reaching age seventeen. The people who made the law must have had some reason for it.

He probably never had to make an effort to learn the church's important prayers such as the Our Father; the Doxology; Come, Holy Spirit; Hail Mary; and of course "Angel of God, my guardian dear." They taught themselves because he heard adults pray them again and again. He must have been deeply influenced by the fact that adults prayed, and prayed very earnestly. Daily prayer was as much a part of life as running and playing, eating and sleeping. It was as much a matter of course as going to church on Sunday.

A child is not yet ready to enter fully into the church's official liturgical prayer, but it can perceive with all its senses that there is such a prayer, and for the moment that is the crucial thing. Besides, a child can also learn to pray on its own. In fact, it is urgently necessary that it learn to speak with God because otherwise, after growing up, it will have great difficulty in finding the door to personal prayer.

When he was little, prayer could be unbearably boring, especially in the month of October when the rosary was prayed every evening. Then his thoughts wandered, and his imagination produced the most marvelous capers. It was a good thing that he could see by looking at the beads of the rosary how far the prayer had progressed. Oddly enough, he remembers those October evenings fondly; he can still see his parents and siblings sitting in a half circle around Mary's image.

His father was a locomotive engineer. Long before the workday started he prepared everything: pocket watch, route maps, some tools, a washcloth and towel, his pajamas for the night away from home. He took special care with the carbide lamps that were used on the railroad at that time. One day the child accidentally entered his parents' bedroom, and there he found his father kneeling on the floor, probably praying for a trip without accidents. Apparently he did that before every day's work. At that time the child knew nothing about it, and he could never forget the image of his father kneeling beside the bed. It was better than a thousand sermons.

☙

As an altar boy he had to know the prayers of the Mass by heart, especially the Prayers at the Foot of the Altar, which was really a private prayer of the priest and altar servers, spoken in dialogue at the foot of the altar steps before the Mass began.

> *Introibo ad altare Dei,*
> [I will go to the altar of God]

the priest began, and the servers responded:

> *Ad Deum, qui laetificat juventutem meam.*
> [To God, the joy of my youth.]

And so it went on, psalm verse after psalm verse. After the table prayer, it was his first encounter with the Psalms. At that time he did not think about what it meant that God would be his joy from his youth. He was more pleased by the elegant flow of the Latin and that he could recite the Mass prayers without making a mistake. It was only much later that he understood the truth that God had indeed been his joy from youth.

☙

Before the reform of the liturgy the Mass had an appendix analogous to the Prayers at the Foot of the Altar, the so-called "Leonine Prayers," prescribed by Pope Leo XIII in 1884. Returning to the foot of the altar steps, the priest spoke a number of prayers for the freedom of the church. Then he prayed to the archangel Michael to defend the church in battle and to thrust into hell Satan and the all the evil spirits "who prowl about the world seeking the ruin of souls."

He was particularly fond of that prayer, especially because it spoke of "spirits" "prowling about" and of the depths of hell. He was not afraid of "hell." It was all about the "evil spirits." It only occurred to him years later that the curate and many of the faithful thought about Hitler and his followers when they prayed that prayer, asking that God would, through the holy angels, conquer their evil! The Leonine Prayers had a political background from the outset and therefore were ideally suited for praying against Hitler. At that time no one dared say aloud what she or he was thinking, but they could speak, and pray, in code. When the curate repeatedly preached, with great emphasis, on the Fifth Commandment most of the adults were fully aware who was intended by "You shall not kill." The Gestapo's spies knew it too. The curate was put in jail more than once to try to frighten him.

<hr>

At that time the Mass was entirely in Latin, except for the gospel and the sermon, but because the Liturgical Movement had already been active in Europe for a long time many pastors tried to engage the faithful more fully in the course of the Mass. As a makeshift aid there were the so-called "community Masses" in which the Collects and the psalm verses were read in German for the congregation by a "prayer leader" while the priest spoke them quietly in Latin. When he himself became a prayer leader he often had to read liturgical texts aloud on Sundays and weekdays. He must have begun at that time to love the "language" of the Roman Collects and the Psalms.

<hr>

In middle school he had a Latin teacher who was not such a great pedagogue but had an excellent knowledge of ancient literature. She read Greek and Latin texts as if they were in her native tongue. Besides, she was a deeply believing woman. At some point, during a class about Livy and his historical work *Ab urbe condita*, she began to speak about the medieval hymn *Veni, Sancte Spiritus* (Come, Holy Spirit). I don't know what circuitous path brought her there. She asked the flabbergasted class which of them could recite the hymn. Of course none of them could, and so the whole class—Protestants, Catholics, freethinkers, and agnostics—had to learn the Latin text of the hymn by heart before the next class. Why? Because every educated person must be familiar with the most important cultural heritage of Europe. He learned it by heart, and in the process it occurred to him how supple and elegant medieval Latin can be. Since that time he happily and frequently prays this most beautiful of all prayers to the Holy Spirit.

❧

Looking back, he is deeply impressed with what outrageous luck he had. Again and again he was surrounded by people who helped him in his faith and pointed him toward great and beautiful things: first his parents, then his older brother, good pastors, and many, many others. Outrageous luck? When his mother died he found a slip of paper in her prayer book on which she had written a sentence from one of Paul's letters: "What do you have that you did not receive?" (1 Cor 4:7), and below it, apparently from Georges Bernanos's *Diary of a Country Priest*, "All is grace."

❧

When he was sixteen he began to keep a diary, but what he wrote down were not his own impressions, and certainly not outpourings of his heart; rather, he copied out texts from books and periodicals that spoke to him or that he found to be unusual. One day he wrote down the famous poem by Teresa of Ávila:

| Let nothing trouble you; | *Nada te turbe,* |
|---|---|
| let nothing frighten you; | *nada te espante,* |
| everything changes | *todo se pasa,* |
| but God does not. | *Dios no se muda.* |
| [Through] patience | *La paçiencia* |
| you will obtain everything; | *todo lo alcanza* |
| whoever has God lacks nothing; | *quien a Dios tiene nada la falta;* |
| [having] only God is enough. | *solo Dios basta.* |

Sometimes when he is feeling miserable and everything is going badly he recites this text. It is the work of a great woman and has nothing to do with despising the world; it is about the faithfulness of God.

⁕

Prayer by no means functions only to put people's spiritual lives in order and give them an inner focus, no matter how important that aspect of prayer can be. It is more than that. It is only when people speak to God that God becomes a real counterpart, that is, a person.

Imagine what it would be like if a married couple lived in the same dwelling, each doing his or her specific tasks—working, cooking, eating—but never speaking to each other. No "good morning," no "good night," no "eat up," no "thank you," no "please." That would be creepy; besides, no one could maintain such an attitude because it would reduce the other person to a nonperson. She or he would be nothing but an object, a kind of machine, a robot. A human being truly becomes a person only when someone looks at her or him with joy, and that joy has to be uttered. If there is no living dialogue between God and a human person, no complaint, no petition, no thanksgiving, God can never be a living person—and so, in the end, will not exist.

⁕

Daily prayer is like a seismograph: when something is not right in his life, he cannot really pray.

⁕

Both are necessary: the church's official liturgical prayer, with its objectivity, and a very personal talking with God that can be altogether subjective. The two kinds of prayer augment each other and lead to each other. In the ideal case they are one.

⁕

He read somewhere that when there is a sudden danger of death a Christian should say a swift prayer of repentance and offer her or his soul to God. At eighteen he found that idea to be right, but he was thrown hard against the ground of reality when, during a mountain hike, he suddenly lost his grip and fell. The only thought that went through his mind in that moment was "I'm falling!"

It all turned out well; he found something to hold on to. Afterward he was so enraged at himself and his carelessness that he didn't even think to thank God. The fall taught him that we shouldn't depend on last-minute repentance; it's better if our repenting starts somewhat sooner.

In 1954, Michel Quoist published a book of prayers and meditations simply entitled *Prières* (*Prayers*).[3] It was quickly translated into other languages, and in Germany alone it achieved more than sixty printings. It was the beginning of a completely new kind of meditative literature containing very personal prayers reflecting real life. To take one example:

> Good-bye, Sir, excuse me, I haven't time.
> I'll come back, I can't wait, I haven't time.
> I must end this letter—I haven't time.
> I can't accept, having no time.
> I can't think, I can't read, I'm swamped, I haven't time.
> I'd like to pray, but I haven't time.
> . . .
> And so all . . . run after time, Lord.
> They pass through life running—hurried, jostled, overburdened,
>     frantic, and they never get there. They haven't time.
> In spite of all their efforts they're still short of time,
> Of a great deal of time.
> Lord, you must have made a mistake in your calculations.
> There is a big mistake somewhere.
> The hours are too short,

3. English: Michel Quoist, *Prayers*, trans. Agnes M. Forsyth and Anne Marie de Commaile (Lanham, MD: Sheed & Ward, 1963).

The days are too short,
Our lives are too short.

You who are beyond time, Lord, you smile to see us fighting it.
And you know what you are doing.
You make no mistakes in your distribution of time to [human
beings].
You give each one time to do what you want him to do.
But we must not lose time
   waste time,
   kill time,
For time is a gift that you give us,
But a perishable gift,
A gift that does not keep.

Lord, I have time, I have plenty of time,
All the time that you give me,
The years of my life,
The days of my years,
The hours of my days,
They are all mine.
Mine to fill, quietly, calmly,
But to fill completely, up to the brim,
To offer them to you, that of their insipid water
   You may make a rich wine such as you made once in Cana
     of Galilee.

I am not asking you tonight, Lord, for time to do this and then
   that,
But your grace to do conscientiously, in the time that you give
   me, what you want me to do.[4]

At the time he was fascinated by this new way of praying. He read
these books over and over, talked about them, gave them as gifts.
For a time this kind of prayer literature was a great help to him,
as it no doubt was for others, and yet he can no longer deal with
such prayers. He couldn't pray that way anymore.

Prayers should indeed be spirit-filled, but they should not be
"spiritual." They have no need to explore beautiful thoughts and

---

4. Ibid., 97–99.

most certainly should not kindle fireworks out of familiar formulas. They are not for spiritual enjoyment; they are an appeal to the holy God. Here again we can learn from the Psalter: while the Psalms speak in a very beautiful and often moving language they always remain simple and direct.

◈

For him, however, there are two exceptions to what he has just said: Augustine's *Confessions* and Karl Rahner's *Encounters with Silence*. He has learned much from both books, and still does. He reads both of them prayerfully, again and again.

> Great are You, O Lord, and greatly to be praised; great is Your power, and of Your wisdom there is no end. And man, being a part of Your creation, desires to praise You—man, who bears about with him his mortality, the witness of his sin, even the witness that You resist the proud—yet man, this part of Your creation, desires to praise You. You move us to delight in praising You; for You have made us for Yourself, and our hearts are restless until they rest in You. (Augustine, *Confessions* 1.1)[5]

> I should like to speak with You, my God, and yet what else can I speak of but You? Indeed, could anything at all exist which had not been present with You from all eternity, which didn't have its true home and most intimate explanation in Your mind and heart? Isn't everything I ever say really a statement about You?
> On the other hand, if I try, shyly and hesitantly, to speak to You about Yourself, You will still be hearing about *me*. For what could I say about You except that You are *my* God, the God of my beginning and end, God of my joy and my need, God of my life?[6]

◈

5. Text available at http://www.newadvent.org/fathers/110101.htm.
6. Karl Rahner, *Encounters with Silence*, 2nd ed., trans. James M. Demske (South Bend, IN: St. Augustine's Press, 1999), 3.

At some point he noticed that most of his prayers had a hidden substructure. The formula was something like this: "O Lord, please will what I want!" Of course, he never formulated it quite that way, but the structure was clearly there, and when he understood that he experienced a Copernican shift. Certainly it did not end with this "insight" into his most secret intentions. He will have to struggle his whole life long not to make God the recipient of his petitions and desires and yoke God to his own interests.

❧

In the course of their lives many Christians have the overwhelming, even terrifying realization of how precisely and more than generously God hears their prayers. The experience is what it is; there is no point in trying to argue or experiment with it; it certainly can't be marketed. It can only be received anew by individuals, Christian communities, or the whole church.

But at the same time—and just as terrifying—there is the experience of God's silence, God's non-intervention, God's seeming to do exactly the opposite of what was asked.

The two experiences cannot be weighed or played off against each other, and those who have had both of them again and again would never even think of doing such a thing, because they have often found that God is present even when silent, that God does not hear prayers and yet does hear them in some other way, and that the very act of petitioning can become a liberating, meaning-bestowing change because the one praying is personally transformed in prayer, and thereby the world itself has been changed for her or him.

❧

In the past he often confessed that he had prayed inattentively. In the meantime he has found that confession inappropriate. It is just something to fill out a confession, all too often replacing the acknowledgment of our real sins: hatred, egoism, lying, hypocrisy, pleasure at the misery of others, greed, hard-heartedness. None of us can control the wandering of our thoughts. Complete attention can only be brief, and God does not desire any kind of mental acrobatics. It suffices to turn one's thoughts to God *before* praying and to say: "Now I want to be wholly with you and nowhere else." And when our mercurial imaginations quickly fly away, we calmly haul them back and continue our prayer without worrying about it. What makes prayer to be prayer is not its perfect form and most certainly not any spiritual enjoyment: it is the will to pray. Those who *want* to pray and open their hearts to it are already praying.

Moreover, our concentration in prayer reflects the way we focus on our work: those who in their daily work are fully attentive to the matter at hand will find it easier to be with God in prayer as well.

❧

There can be no discrepancy between an active life and frequent prayer. Medieval theology had already observed that *ex abundantia contemplationis activus* [action arises from an abundance of contemplation]. We could expand the statement: those who work seriously pray all the better, and those who pray with pure hearts drag God into action. Anyone who does not believe that should consider the lives of the great saints: for example, Teresa of Ávila (1515–1582). She was a master of internal prayer, and she founded no fewer than fifteen monasteries for women (often in the face of tremendous external resistance).

❧

Unfortunately, it took rather a long time before he recognized the connection between prayer and committed work. He was aided by a poem from the Swedish author Hedvig Fornander (1937–1989), which says in part:

> It is not the eye that knows
> but the back, which bears the burden.

❧

In the "First German Mass" by Johann Michael Haydn (1737–1806), the younger brother of Joseph Haydn, the entrance song reads:

Here lies before your majesty,
in dust, the mass of Christians,
lifting its heart to you, O God,
its eyes toward the altar.
O Father, bestow your favor!
Forgive our guilt and sin!
O God, never banish us poor sinners
from before Thy face.[7]

While this German Mass is still sung, the whole of it has long
since been dropped from the official hymnals. The entrance hymn
itself is scarcely bearable any longer. At any rate, it does not succeed in making us feel that we are lying "in dust" before the divine "majesty." All the same, the concepts used in it are not so
unbiblical as they might seem. This entrance hymn was intended
to express in the language of its own time something that is indispensable: the adoration a believer owes to God and that has been
so encumbered in today's worship services with their superabun-
dance of instruction and didactic tomfoolery.

Sometimes he has a longing, even during the Mass, to be able
to worship silently with his whole existence, without words.

Fey von Hassell, daughter of the resistance fighter Ulrich von Hassell, who was hanged by the Nazis because of his participation
in the unsuccessful attack on Hitler on 20 July 1944, writes in her
book *Niemals sich beugen*:[8]

We sat at long tables pushed together in the form of horseshoes.
Before we sat down we had to hold hands and roar, more than
shout: "I'm hungry." After the meal we stood up and roared:
"I'm full."[9]

---

7. Translation LMM.

8. English: *Hostage of the Third Reich: The Story of my Imprisonment and Rescue
from the SS*, trans. David Forbes-Wall (New York: Scribner, 1989).

9. Translation LMM.

When he read the book he marked that passage. For him the scene Fey von Hassell describes is not only repulsive but also shows him the high quality of Christian table manners. Both Jews and Christians, by their table prayers, defend a meal culture that is infinitely superior to such barbarity.

❧

He became aware relatively late of the *ecclesial* dimension of any kind of prayer. I am not referring to prayers for the pope, the bishops, the church as a whole. He had been familiar with those for a long time. No, I mean something more: namely, that every prayer, even the most intimate and personal, happens *in communio* with the church because the individual praying is a member of the Body of Christ, and without the Spirit of Christ, who ensouls the church, no individual would be able to pray.

He can no longer overlook the fact that the Psalms shift so often between the "I" of the one praying and the "I" of Israel and that Jesus formulated the Our Father entirely as a prayer from "us."

❧

The older he gets, the less he understands the hesitation of his Protestant fellow Christians to engage with Mary in prayer as well. Certainly she is not "adored," but she is "called upon." That is a difference as wide as the heavens.

He also speaks with his dead mother, tells her what is affecting him, reminds her of days past, asks for her help. That is quite common in a family, and yet in both Protestantism and Catholicism we confess our belief in the *familia Dei,* the family of God, and in the *communio sanctorum,* the communion of saints.

❧

He cannot deny that there were times in his life when he did not pray at all. He never decided not to do it; it simply crept in. But so did the consequences: days lost their shape, things lost their shine. Ugliness became still more ugly; conflicts with others in the house piled up. The times without prayer were the worst in his life.

In 1 Thessalonians, Paul writes that the faithful should pray "without ceasing" (1 Thess 5:17; cp. Luke 18:1; Rom 12:12; Eph 6:18; Col 4:2). What did he mean by that? Most certainly not that the Christians in Thessalonica should fill up the whole day with prayers. The immediately preceding statement is: "Rejoice always!" That too certainly cannot mean that they should smile at every moment. This is about a basic current that should sustain their lives: joy at the nearness of Christ. Something similar must then be true of prayer: gratitude for what God had done in them should fill the lives of all Christians. That gratitude can be expressed in many ways: a song, a psalm, a brief glance toward God. We can make it a habit to thank God for everything we encounter—a piece of news, a beautiful object, or the dear face of another person.

And yet at times he asks himself whether he is capable of praising God at all. Isn't his praise more of a self-assurance, self-affirmation, self-exaltation—and thus a kind of hygiene of the soul that, while it is highly effective (quite obviously!) has nothing to do with God? Can it be that all his praying is nothing but a kind of corset for sustaining his inner calm because, after all, people need familiar customs and rituals? At such times he can only pray with Psalm 51: "O Lord, open my lips, and my mouth will declare your praise." Of and by ourselves we are absolutely incapable of praising God.

The author of Ephesians writes, in his admonitions that close the book:

> Pray in the Spirit at all times in every prayer and supplication. To that end keep alert and always persevere in supplication for all the saints. Pray also for me. (Eph 6:18-19)

These few lines contain a whole theology of prayer. It is preceded by the well-known description of the armor of salvation: the Christian is in combat with evil, armed like a Roman foot soldier with belt, breastplate, shoes, shield, helmet, and sword. The little catechesis on prayer is directly connected to this description. That is: prayer is part of the Christian's battle in faith, and it can be a battle of its own. As a soldier must keep alert, so must the believer in prayer. One may not ease up; one must constantly be ready, praying at all times.

But in addition there is a theme that plays an astonishingly large role in the New Testament letters: supplication for "all the saints," that is, for all fellow Christians, the whole community. For Paul and his disciples a prayer in which one prays only for oneself or cultivates a personal relationship with God is unthinkable. Every prayer, to be genuine, requires a radical openness to fellow Christians and their common calling.

It is from this point of view that we should understand prayer "in the Spirit" in the quoted text. The author of Ephesians is familiar with Pauline theology and therefore knows that, when we pray, the Holy Spirit we received in baptism is beseeching in us. But this author is also aware that the same Spirit binds all the baptized in one Body. That is why "praying in the Spirit" necessarily means praying *with* and *for* the church.

*

When he was about twenty-five he read *The Way of a Pilgrim*,[10] and since then the little book has a place of honor in his library. It promotes the Eastern Church tradition of the Jesus Prayer, repeating over and over again in the same rhythm the petition of the blind man outside Jericho (Mark 10:48): "Jesus, Son of David, have mercy on me!" In reading that little book he realized that, oddly enough, there are virtually no set, familiar prayers of private devotion in the Western Church that are addressed directly to Jesus. The book appealed to him very strongly at that time because it did not instruct but simply told. It begins:

10. See *The Way of a Pilgrim*, translated from Russian by Olga Savin (Boston: Shambhala Publications, 2001).

By the grace of God I am a Christian man, by my own actions a great sinner, and by calling a homeless wanderer of the humblest origins, roaming from place to place. My worldly belongings consist of a knapsack on my back, containing some dried bread, and a Holy Bible in my breast pocket. That is all.

On the twenty-fourth Sunday after Pentecost I went to church to worship at the Liturgy. During the reading of the Epistle of Saint Paul to the Thessalonians [1 Thess. 5:17] I heard the following words: "Pray without ceasing." This verse especially fixed itself in my mind, and I began to wonder how one could pray unceasingly, since each man must occupy himself with other matters as well, in order to make a living. I checked in the Bible and read with my own eyes that which I had already heard: namely, that one should "pray without ceasing," "pray at all times in the Spirit" [Eph. 6:18], and "in all places pray with uplifted hands" [1 Tim. 2:8]. I thought about this for some time but was unable to understand it.[11]

The story that follows tells how the pilgrim travels farther and farther and finds his way to unceasing prayer. The little book had a significance for the faithful in Russia very similar to the influence in the West of the *Imitation of Christ*, attributed to Thomas à Kempis.

When he had read *The Way of a Pilgrim* with great curiosity and fascination he himself tried the Jesus Prayer but soon abandoned it. Still, it returned from time to time, and now he often prays it. There are many opportunities during the day to repeat that appeal anew. It reduces the many words we often speak to God to a single sentence. It creates a place within the complex spaces of our world that is very simple and links us directly to Jesus.

❧

Prayer is not magical. There are times, again and again, when he is helpless and cannot discover what God wants from him. There are also times when he is discouraged or simply cannot understand why God has imposed this or that on him. No angel descends from heaven; no dreams like those related in the Bible tell him what

11. Ibid., 1.

he should do; no inner enlightenment explodes in his thoughts. But it may be that God's silence drives him to open himself to his sisters and brothers in the community, to ask their advice, and to be humble enough finally to let others help him. It may be that it is precisely in this way that God wants to speak to him.

※

The Jesus prayer or the rosary may have the outward form of a mantra, but in their internal structure they are altogether different from a continually repeated "Rama, Rama, Rama" or "Om mani padme hum" or other mantras, for they are not a structure to promote concentration, as in Buddhism, not the words of an ego seeking internal communication with its higher ego, not the search for identification with the divine primal grounding of the world. Rather, they are appeals to an Other who is in no way one's own self or the essence of the world or a diffuse divinity. Certainly, Hindu mantras can also appeal to a particular deity, but the one called on in the Jesus Prayer is a historical person. The one who speaks the Jesus Prayer enters into a real history: calling, with blind Bartimaeus, to Jesus as he approaches Jerusalem and asking for his help. Those who pray the rosary most certainly enter into the life of Jesus and its phases. Both Jews and Christians, when they pray, are always dealing with the living God who has spoken, acted, liberated, and redeemed in the midst of this our history.

※

One day, while reading a book by the theologian Otto Hermann Pesch, he came across the expression "narrative prayer." By that Pesch means: something has taken place before my eyes or has happened to me; now it is working on me. It fills up my consciousness. I can't forget about it. So I simply tell it to God, as I would tell a good friend about it.

> Could not simple telling be a form that corresponds to the unadorned and factual character of prayer today, and that nevertheless brings the whole variety of life before God?

.  .  .

> I cannot pray narratively without thus drawing God into the
> midst of my life. When I pray by "telling" I address God, count
> on God's presence, believe that God hears me, that I have some-
> thing to do with God, that I am "interesting" to God.[12]

The expression "narrative prayer" was entirely new to him, but he
was very familiar with the thing itself. Hadn't he often lamented
his suffering to God by listing all sorts of things, telling his tale of
misery? And, on the other hand, hadn't he often spoken to God
about his joys, listing what had given him so much pleasure and
in the process giving thanks to God?

Then he remembered having read something similar in the great
instructors in the spiritual life: we should imagine Jesus alive,
always have him present to us, tell him everything that affects
us, and ask him for help when we don't know how to go on. He
finds the idea of "narrative prayer" helpful. It opens up for him
a form of prayer that is possible for us at any time.

❦

One day he came across Mark 11:25 and discovered the passage
anew:

> Whenever you stand praying, forgive, if you have anything
> against anyone, so that your Father in heaven may also forgive
> you your trespasses.

He had always let that rush past him, as one does with religious
texts. The world is full of rushing. But now he suddenly read with
different eyes and saw the revolutionary statement: He dare not
even begin to pray without first making certain of his relationship to the people around him. Who is he avoiding? Whom does
he not want to see? Whom does he mistrust? Who is profoundly

---

12. Otto Hermann Pesch, *Das Gebet* (Mainz: Matthias-Grünewald, 1980). Translation LMM.

disagreeable to him? Who evokes certain memories in him, things he simply cannot forget? Whom can he not forgive?

If he took such reflection seriously he would not get around to prayer very soon—and yet that very preparation for prayer would change the world a bit.

※

It would be dangerous to pray, or to talk about the right way to pray, without recalling again and again the words of Jesus that are so hard that they cut every Christian to the quick:

> Why do you call me "Lord, Lord!" and do not do what I tell you? (Luke 6:46)

That infinitely sober question from the Sermon on the Plain remains a corrective that must accompany all Christian prayer.

※

He has known people who were altogether devoted to their work in service to the church. They were tireless in helping to build up communities; they did what needed to be done without saying much about it; they were conscientious even about details and at the same time were always friendly and ready to help. In the words of the gospels they were like "worthless slaves" (cp. Luke 17:10) who did not forfeit their reward.

He suspects that for them, even if they did not put it that way, work was prayer. And in that connection he thinks of Georges Bernanos's *Diary of a Country Priest*, from which he at some point copied this passage:

> "Go on with your work," he said. "Keep at the little daily things that need doing, till the rest comes. Concentrate. Think of a lad at his homework, trying so hard and his tongue sticking out. That's how Our Lord would have us be when He gives us up to our own strength. Little things—they don't look much, yet they bring peace. Like wild flowers which seem to have no scent, till

you get a field full of 'em. And he who prays for little things—is innocent.[13]

❧

There were times when he tried to stop praying for personal things, but then it always became clear to him how wrong that would be. After all, asking God for something always means: "I can't do it myself. I need help—in fact, I need help in everything." In view of the creatureliness of humans, petition is so elementary that doing without it over a long time would damage every baptized person.

This is not to say that there cannot be phases in Christian existence when personal petition is less frequent and may even fall silent for a while—just as there are phases in which the person praying senses how inadequate are all the words one says to God. But such experiences are usually part of a long history of prayer in which very concrete petitions that ask for things and make claims before God are primary, and such phases may recur very often.

❧

It would be tragic if, at the end of this book, readers had the impression that they need to stuff their days full with spiritual exercises and every possible kind of prayer—praise, thanksgiving, petition, lament, adoration, meditation—and at the same time not forget to pray in turn to God the Father, Jesus Christ, and the Holy Spirit. That would be a dreadful misunderstanding.

Here, as in all things, the fact is that there is a time for everything! There are days on which we would like more than anything to be dancing, and there are times of prayer and of deep lament. There are periods of spiritual dryness, and sometimes even hours in which God fills our hearts with overwhelming joy. There are even times in which we want to be silent before God because we

---

13. Georges Bernanos, *The Diary of a Country Priest*, trans. Pamela Morris (New York: Macmillan, 1937), 209.

are weary with our many words. Besides, we ought always to pray as the Spirit of God leads us.

＊

All the same, for many years he has prayed his Psalms every day, and for good reason: namely, that despite all Christian freedom there is a "basic ration" of daily prayer that we need to maintain. It is different for each person. For him it is the daily Psalms. For Jews it is the *Shema*, "Hear, O Israel!" and the long *amidah*, the Eighteen Benedictions recited three times a day. The one who prays must never subtract from such a basic standard. It is *officium*, thus "obligation," "what is owed," "service," whether we feel like it or not. It is especially when he has no appetite for it that his prayer is serious and truly honors God.

＊

Sometimes he prays that in his last hour he will still have the strength to lay his many years, indeed his whole existence, in the hands of God. Of course, he knows that it is not accomplished just by asking, but he has to begin today.

# Resources

*For the Psalms, see especially:*

Hossfeld, Frank-Lothar, and Erich Zenger. *Psalms 2 (Psalms 51–100)*. Translated by Linda M. Maloney. Hermeneia. Minneapolis: Fortress Press, 2005.

———. *Psalms 3 (Psalms 101–150)*. Translated by Linda M. Maloney. Hermeneia. Minneapolis: Fortress Press, 2011.

Lohfink, Norbert. *In the Shadow of Your Wings: New Readings of Great Texts from the Bible*. Translated by Linda M. Maloney. Collegeville, MN: Liturgical Press, 2003.

———. *Option for the Poor: The Basic Principle of Liberation Theology in the Light of the Bible*. Translated by Linda M. Maloney. Berkeley: BIBAL Press, 1987.

Zenger, Erich. "New Approaches to the Study of the Psalms." *Proceedings of the Irish Biblical Association* 17 (1994): 37–54.

*For the Our Father, see:*

Lohfink, Gerhard. *The Our Father: A New Reading*. Translated by Linda M. Maloney. Collegeville, MN: Liturgical Press, 2018.